Good Housekeeping

Budget Dinners

Quick & Easy Everyday Recipes

HEARST BOOKS

A division of Sterling Publishing Co., Inc.

New York / London
www.sterlingpublishing.com

ALL RECIPES
· GOOD ·
HOUSEKEEPING
Since ★ 1909
COOKBOOKS
Triple TESTED

This custom edition published by
World Publications Group, Inc.
140 Laurel Street
East Bridgewater, MA 02333
www.wrldpub.com

Originally published by Hearst Books in a different format as *Good Housekeeping Budget Dinners!*

Copyright © 2010 by Hearst Communications, Inc.

Book design by Memo Productions
Edited by Sarah Scheffel

Photography Credits
Front cover Kate Sears
Back cover James Baigrie

Interior
Quentin Bacon 72

James Baigrie 6, 23, 24, 33, 35, 41, 45, 49, 51, 52, 96, 99, 103, 105, 133

Monica Buck 4, 61, 67, 106, 119

Beatriz Da Costa 81

Brian Hagiwara 7, 27, 38, 75, 78, 85, 127, 136, 139, 148

Lisa Hubbard 88, 91

Frances Janisch 131

Rita Maas 20

Kate Mathis 95

Steven Mark Needham 111

Ngoc Minh Ngo 93

Con Poulos 71

David Prince 10, 17

Alan Richardson 143, 145

Kate Sears 54, 56

Amy Kalyn Sims 63

Ann Stratton 112

Mark Thomas 87, 115, 123, 140

The Good Housekeeping Seal guarantees that the recipes in this cookbook meet the strict standards of the Good Housekeeping Research Institute. The Institute has been a source of reliable information and a consumer advocate since 1900, and established its seal of approval in 1909. Every recipe has been triple-tested for ease, reliability, and great taste.

Hearst Books
A Division of Sterling Publishing Co., Inc.
387 Park Avenue South
New York, NY 10016

Good Housekeeping is a registered trademark of Hearst Communications, Inc.

www.goodhousekeeping.com

Manufactured in China

ISBN 978-1-57215-618-0

10 9 8 7 6 5 4 3 2 1

CONTENTS

Butternut Squash
Lasagna (page 60)

FOREWORD

When we're developing recipes at *Good Housekeeping,* we're always factoring time and cost. In this diverse collection of more than 100 recipes, we want to show you that it's possible—actually easy—to prepare delicious, family-friendly meals on a budget. With your convenience in mind, we've organized *Budget Dinners!* by strategies. Instead of classic chapters like Beef and Poultry, you'll find eight roads into feeding your family frugally, from "Cook It Slow and Easy" to "Cheap Grills."

What could be more economical than taking a tough cut of meat and simmering it until it's tender and succulent? We've used the slow cooker to update classics like Coq au Vin and added simple new recipes like Chinese-inspired Red-Cooked Turkey Thighs. When you have a busy week ahead, consider "One Dish, Many Meals." With this strategy, you'll prepare Pot Roast with Fall Vegetables, for example, and have enough leftovers for two additional suppers—Brisket Sandwiches and Easy Spaghetti Bolognese.

Whether you make an omelet or Savory Ricotta Pancakes, breakfast for dinner is always a treat. And our pasta suppers—including Sausage and Pepper Baked Ziti and Chicken Bolognese—feed the gang inexpensively, too. Soothe your family with a big hearty pot of soup, or challenge them to go vegetarian for a night. Our meatless meals are so satisfying, they'll be begging for tasty Southwestern Black-Bean Burgers. Our strategies finish with "Supper in a Salad Bowl," always healthful and affordable, and "Cheap Grills," because our readers frequently ask for ways to make grilling more economical.

Armed with these recipes—and our wallet-friendly tips sprinkled throughout the pages—you'll get more mileage out of your food budget. So go shopping, start cooking, and enjoy home-cooked dinners with your family and friends!

SUSAN WESTMORELAND
Food Director, *Good Housekeeping*

INTRODUCTION

"What's for dinner?" is a question every home cook must address each and every day. We want to serve nutritious, delicious meals that our families will love, and we want to do so on a sensible budget with a minimum amount of fuss. But when you consider that a home-cooked supper costs the typical American family of four about $5 per person, these perfectly reasonable goals can seem daunting. And rising prices for staples like eggs, milk, and wheat products can make them seem more daunting still.

Take heart: At *Good Housekeeping*, we have the same goals and concerns that you do, and we are determined to beat the trends. That's why we've pulled together this carefully selected collection of recipes to help you spend less and eat better. This book is all about smart, family-friendly meal-time strategies: eight of them, to be precise.

Looking for dinnertime solutions sure to please each and every family member? Try our all-time favorite slow-cooker suppers, breakfast for dinner, and our recommendations for grilling on a budget. Want to maximize leftovers? We'll teach you how to give suppers a second and even a *third* act. Got a lot of mouths to feed? Our soup pot is never empty and there's always enough pasta to feed your crowd. Do you believe that health and wealth go hand-in-hand? Try our main-dish salads or eat vegetarian for a night (we've selected recipes so tempting no one will ask "Where's the meat?").

In total, this book provides more than 100 low-cost, full-flavor recipes—including delicious meals for under $10—that go beyond the usual inexpensive (but boring) tuna casserole and spaghetti with marinara sauce. Serve our Butternut Squash Lasagna, Baked Eggs with Polenta and Chunky Vegetable Sauce (see photo, opposite), Turkey and White Bean Chili, Pastrami-Spiced Flank Steak (see photo, below), and Slow-Cooked Pulled Pork, and no will even suspect that you're making your dollars holler!

Wallet-friendly tips on shopping and cooking plus a two-week menu planner make *Budget Dinners!* a practical resource for every family cook. Advice on freezing everything (from ingredients to finished dishes) plus smart ideas for using all sorts of leftovers make it a truly indispensable meal-planning guide. As always, each delicious recipe has been triple-tested (and triple-tasted!) in the *Good Housekeeping* kitchens.

BUDGET-SAVVY SHOPPING TIPS

Below are general guidelines that will help keep you on budget as you navigate your way through the grocery store aisles. Throughout the book, we've supplied additional tips to help stretch your dollars at the supermarket.

Buy in bulk, especially for dry goods. See our thoughts on the benefits of beans (page 33) and whole grains (page 87).

Seek out sales on produce. And shop for fruits and vegetables that are in season, when they're usually less expensive. Visit farmers' markets and stalls to shop for produce grown locally. (See also Wallet-Friendly Tips: High-Yield Harvests, page 85).

Avoid purchasing prepared main meals. And steer away from prerinsed salad greens and sliced vegetables. When choosing packaged goods, compare cost per volume. (For help, see What Convenience Costs, page 150.)

Opt for dried versions of foods like pasta and herbs. (For recipes, see Strategy 5: Pasta for Your Crowd, page 54.)

Cheaper cuts of meat can be a good choice, and buying the whole bird is always the thriftiest option. Just be sure to select the correct method for cooking whatever cut you bring home. See Wallet-Friendly Tips for Meat (page 139) and Poultry (page 145).

Consider the benefits of soy products, to your waistline and your pocketbook. (See Wallet-Friendly Tips: Soy, page 81.)

Prefer to start your day with scrambled eggs and cheese? See our advice on shopping for dairy products, pages 95 and 99.

Avoid impulse purchases (and going to the store when you're hungry!). That way, you're more likely to buy only what you'll use.

Invest in high-quality, airtight storage containers or freezer-weight self-sealing plastic bags to ensure the longevity and safety of food. See our tips on choosing and storing fresh herbs (page 59), fresh greens (page 63), and potatoes (page 119).

WALLET-FRIENDLY COOKING TIPS

Our thrifty ideas don't stop at the grocery-store checkout counter. The following suggestions will help you save money *after* you get your groceries home.

Map out the week's meals after you shop so you can make the best use of all the fresh ingredients you bought on sale. Need help? See our Two-Week Budget Menu Planner (page 154) before you head for the store.

Select a heavy cooking pot with a tight-fitting lid to prevent evaporation and loss of flavor and volume. Slow cookers are a great option: See Strategy 1: Cook It Slow and Easy, page 10.

While canned broths are convenient, having a supply of homemade stock in the freezer is worth the few weekend hours it takes as it simmers. For recipes, see Chicken Broth (page 108) and Turkey Broth (page 53).

Make your own dry rubs, marinades, seasoning mixes, and salad dressings. For a simple vinaigrette recipe, see Side Salad in a Snap, page 43.

In season, freeze chopped tomatoes, peppers, celery, or green onions in ½ cup amounts. Add them, still frozen, to sauces, soups, and stews. (See How to Freeze Anything, page 152.)

We hate to waste food. That's why we share lots of creative ideas for giving leftovers a second act. For starters, see Fast Ways to Make Over Leftovers, page 30.

When preparing meals, double the recipe and freeze half for a busy evening when you might be tempted to buy expensive prepared food or takeout. For tips, see Freeze Now, Serve Later Casseroles (page 69) and Soups and Stews (page 109). Or check out our triple-threat recipes in Strategy 2: One Dish, Many Meals, page 24.

STRATEGY 1:
COOK IT SLOW & EASY

Nothing makes dinner prep easier than the original fix-it-and-forget-it appliance, the slow cooker. You simply add your ingredients first thing in the morning, and your home-cooked dinner will be ready and waiting by the end of the day—so convenient. Plus, slow cooking allows meats to become their most tender (including tougher, cheaper cuts of meat), vegetables to fully absorb stocks and spices, and flavors to develop to their fullest. It's a great choice for any soups, stews, or chilis you'd typically cook on a stovetop.

Since the food is cooked slowly at low temperatures, this method is also efficient at retaining essential vitamins and minerals. What's more, a slow cooker is more energy efficient than a conventional oven; in fact, a well-functioning slow cooker should use about the same amount of electricity as a lightbulb. For all of these reasons, we're celebrating slow cooking as our first tried-and-true "dinner on a budget" strategy.

In this chapter we present a selection of our most delicious and affordable slow cooker recipes. From homey comfort food to mouth-watering dishes featuring exotic spices and flavors, slow cooking is one-pot cooking at its simple best. For optimum results, be sure to check out our Go Slow tips on page 13 before you begin.

Chicken Tagine (page 19)

SLOW-COOKED PULLED PORK

Pork shoulder blade roast is known as a cheap cut of meat. But when slow-cooked for hours in a sweet and tangy sauce, it becomes meltingly tender.

ACTIVE TIME: 20 MINUTES · **TOTAL TIME:** 8 HOURS
MAKES: 12 MAIN-DISH SERVINGS

---

1   MEDIUM ONION, CHOPPED

½   CUP KETCHUP

⅓   CUP CIDER VINEGAR

¼   CUP PACKED BROWN SUGAR

¼   CUP TOMATO PASTE

2   TABLESPOONS SWEET PAPRIKA

2   TABLESPOONS WORCESTERSHIRE SAUCE

2   TABLESPOONS YELLOW MUSTARD

1½ TEASPOONS SALT

1¼ TEASPOONS GROUND BLACK PEPPER

4   POUND BONELESS PORK SHOULDER BLADE ROAST (FRESH PORK BUTT), CUT INTO 4 PIECES

12 SOFT SANDWICH BUNS OR CIABATTA ROLLS, WARMED

DILL PICKLES (OPTIONAL)

POTATO CHIPS (OPTIONAL)

HOT SAUCE (OPTIONAL)

1   In 4½- to 6-quart slow-cooker pot, stir onion, ketchup, vinegar, brown sugar, tomato paste, paprika, Worcestershire, mustard, salt, and pepper until combined. Add pork to sauce mixture and turn to coat well with sauce.

2   Cover slow cooker with lid and cook pork mixture on low setting as manufacturer directs, 8 to 10 hours or until pork is very tender.

3   With tongs, transfer pork to large bowl. Turn setting on slow cooker to high; cover and heat sauce to boiling to thicken and reduce slightly.

4   While sauce boils, with two forks, pull pork into shreds. Return shredded pork to slow cooker and toss with sauce to combine. Cover slow cooker and heat through on high setting if necessary.

5   Spoon pork mixture onto bottom of sandwich buns; replace tops of buns. Serve sandwiches with pickles, potato chips, and hot sauce, if you like.

EACH SERVING: ABOUT 475 CALORIES | 31G PROTEIN | 29G CARBOHYDRATE | 26G TOTAL FAT (9G SATURATED) | 2G FIBER | 107MG CHOLESTEROL | 760MG SODIUM

GO SLOW

Before you try any of our fix-'em-and-forget-'em slow-cooker meals, look over these helpful hints.

Prep the night before, and all you'll have to do in the morning is toss your ingredients into the bowl and flip the switch. To do: Measure ingredients, cut vegetables, trim fat from meats. Then refrigerate components separately in bowls or plastic storage bags.

Place root vegetables in the bottom of the slow-cooker bowl, then top with chicken or meat pieces. This way the veggies will be covered by enough stock or sauce to keep them tender—and the meat will be insulated from overcooking.

Never fill the bowl up to the brim—if you do, bubbling-hot liquid may spurt out. For soups and stews, leave about 2 inches of space between food and lid.

Browning chicken or meat before slow cooking is not—we repeat, not—necessary. But if you have the time, it'll give your dish a richer flavor. Avoid using ground meat or poultry in a cooker; low, slow heating makes it a mealy mush.

Resist the urge to take the lid off the cooker and stir the ingredients, especially in the initial stages of warming—the pot will lose valuable heat.

The slow cooker's long-simmer method tends to dissipate the flavor of dried herbs, so adjust seasonings by stirring a little more in at the end of cooking. When using fresh herbs, save some to toss in at the last minute for fresh flavor and color.

During long hours of cooking, milk, sour cream, heavy cream, and cheese break down. For best results, add just before serving.

If the recipe produces more sauce than you want or if the sauce seems too thin, thicken it this way: With a slotted spoon, transfer chicken or meat pieces and vegetables to a serving dish and keep them warm by covering with foil. Turn the slow-cooker dial to high and heat the remaining liquid, uncovered, to reduce to desired thickness—this shouldn't take more than 10 minutes. Next time, remember to start with less liquid (try ½ to 1 cup).

To make cleanup easier, check your supermarket for slow-cooker bowl liners (they fit both round and oval pots). Just be careful to remove food before lifting the liner—it may break if you don't.

LATIN-STYLE BRAISED BEEF

In Spanish, this dish is known as "ropa vieja" (old clothes) because the meat—brisket or another economical cut of beef—is cooked until it's so tender it can be shredded into what resembles a pile of rags.

ACTIVE TIME: 20 MINUTES · **TOTAL TIME:** 9 HOURS
MAKES: 8 MAIN-DISH SERVINGS

---

1 CAN (14½ OUNCES) DICED TOMATOES

1 TABLESPOON CAPERS, DRAINED

1 TABLESPOON GROUND CUMIN

½ TEASPOON GROUND CINNAMON

1 TEASPOON SALT

3 CLOVES GARLIC, SLICED

2 LARGE GREEN, YELLOW, AND/OR RED PEPPERS, SLICED

2 LARGE PICKLED JALAPEÑO CHILES, SLICED

1 MEDIUM ONION, CUT IN HALF AND SLICED

1 FRESH BEEF BRISKET (3 POUNDS)

WARM TORTILLAS AND/OR COOKED WHITE RICE WITH PARSLEY (OPTIONAL)

1 In 4½- to 6-quart slow-cooker bowl, combine tomatoes with their juice, capers, cumin, cinnamon, and salt. Add garlic, peppers, jalapeños, onion, and brisket; stir to coat brisket and vegetables with tomato mixture. Cover slow cooker with lid and cook as manufacturer directs, on low setting 9 to 10 hours or on high setting 6 to 6½ hours.

2 With slotted spoon, transfer brisket and vegetables to large bowl. With two forks, shred brisket with the grain into fine strips. Skim and discard fat from cooking liquid. Stir cooking liquid into brisket mixture. Serve brisket mixture with tortillas and/or rice, if you like.

EACH SERVING: ABOUT 400 CALORIES | 35G PROTEIN | 7G CARBOHYDRATE | 25G TOTAL FAT (9G SATURATED) | 2G FIBER | 109MG CHOLESTEROL | 690MG SODIUM

CORNED BEEF AND CABBAGE

A slow cooker cooks up this budget classic with ease.

ACTIVE TIME: 15 MINUTES · **TOTAL TIME:** 10 HOURS
MAKES: 6 MAIN-DISH SERVINGS

8-INCH SQUARE CHEESECLOTH

12 PARSLEY STEMS

2 CLOVES GARLIC, CRUSHED WITH SIDE OF CHEF'S KNIFE

2 BAY LEAVES

1 TABLESPOON BLACK PEPPERCORNS

1 CORNED BEEF BRISKET (3½ TO 4 POUNDS), FLAT (THIN) CUT

1½ POUNDS SMALL RED POTATOES, UNPEELED AND EACH CUT INTO 1½-INCH CHUNKS

1 POUND CARROTS, CUT INTO 2-INCH PIECES

1 SMALL HEAD GREEN CABBAGE (1½ POUNDS), CUT INTO 8 WEDGES

1 In cheesecloth, wrap parsley, garlic, bay leaves, and peppercorns; tie with string and place in bottom of 5½- to 6-quart slow cooker. Add corned beef; top with potatoes and carrots. Pour in enough *water* to cover meat. Place cabbage on top. Cover slow cooker with lid and cook on low setting as manufacturer directs, 10 to 12 hours or until beef is very tender.
2 To serve, thinly slice corned beef across the grain; transfer to warm large platter with vegetables.

EACH SERVING: ABOUT 440 CALORIES | 27G PROTEIN | 28G CARBOHYDRATE | 25G TOTAL FAT (8G SATURATED) | 125MG CHOLESTEROL | 4G FIBER | 1,480MG SODIUM

CREAMY CHICKEN AND POTATOES

Comfort food was never easier—or more affordable—than this slow-cooked chicken and potato supper.

ACTIVE TIME: 20 MINUTES · **TOTAL TIME:** 8 HOURS
MAKES: 6 MAIN-DISH SERVINGS

---

3 CARROTS (8 OUNCES), PEELED AND CUT INTO ½-INCH SLICES

1 POUND RED POTATOES, EACH CUT INTO QUARTERS

1 SMALL ONION, COARSELY CHOPPED

1 CLOVE GARLIC, CRUSHED WITH PRESS

1 CUT-UP CHICKEN (3½ TO 4 POUNDS), SKIN REMOVED FROM ALL PIECES EXCEPT WINGS

1 CUP CHICKEN BROTH

3 TABLESPOONS CORNSTARCH

½ TEASPOON DRIED THYME

1 TEASPOON SALT

¼ TEASPOON GROUND BLACK PEPPER

1 PACKAGE (10 OUNCES) FROZEN PEAS, THAWED

½ CUP HEAVY WHIPPING CREAM

1 In 5- to 6-quart slow cooker, combine carrots, potatoes, onion, and garlic. Place chicken pieces on top of vegetables. In 2-cup liquid measuring cup, with fork, mix chicken broth, cornstarch, thyme, salt, and pepper; pour mixture over chicken and vegetables. Cover slow cooker with lid and cook as manufacturer directs, on low setting 8 hours or on high setting 6 hours.
2 With tongs or slotted spoon, transfer chicken pieces to warm deep platter. With slotted spoon, transfer vegetables to platter with chicken pieces. Cover platter to keep warm. Stir peas and cream into cooking liquid; heat through. Spoon sauce over chicken and vegetables on platter.

EACH SERVING: ABOUT 380 CALORIES | 36G PROTEIN | 30G CARBOHYDRATE | 12G TOTAL FAT (6G SATURATED) | 4G FIBER | 127MG CHOLESTEROL | 680MG SODIUM

COQ AU VIN

If you're an early riser with extra A.M. time, try this easy, make-ahead slow cooker Coq au Vin. You can even cook extra bacon to munch on for breakfast.

ACTIVE TIME: 20 MINUTES · **TOTAL TIME:** 8 HOURS
MAKES: 4 MAIN-DISH SERVINGS

---

3   SLICES BACON, CUT CROSSWISE INTO ¾-INCH PIECES

1   PACKAGE (10 OUNCES) MUSHROOMS, EACH CUT IN HALF

2   CUPS FROZEN PEARL ONIONS

1   CUT-UP CHICKEN (4 POUNDS), SKIN REMOVED FROM ALL PIECES EXCEPT WINGS

½   TEASPOON SALT

¼   TEASPOON GROUND BLACK PEPPER

1   MEDIUM ONION, CHOPPED

1   LARGE CARROT, CHOPPED

4   CLOVES GARLIC, CHOPPED

1   CUP DRY RED WINE

2   TABLESPOONS TOMATO PASTE

1   BAY LEAF

¾   CUP CHICKEN BROTH

1   In 12-inch nonstick skillet, cook bacon over medium heat until browned. With slotted spoon, transfer bacon to paper towels to drain; set aside.

2   Meanwhile, in 5- to 6-quart slow cooker, combine mushrooms and frozen pearl onions; set aside.

3   Sprinkle chicken pieces with salt and black pepper. In skillet with bacon fat, cook chicken (in 2 batches, if necessary) over medium-high heat until browned, about 10 minutes. Place chicken over vegetables in slow cooker.

4   Discard drippings from skillet. Reduce heat to medium; add onion and carrot, and cook 2 minutes or until onion softens, stirring frequently. Stir in garlic and cook 1 minute. Add wine, tomato paste, and bay leaf; heat to boiling, stirring to dissolve tomato paste. Pour wine mixture and broth over chicken pieces. Cover slow cooker and cook as manufacturer directs, on low setting 8 hours or on high setting 4 hours.

5   To serve, discard bay leaf. With large spoon, transfer chicken and sauce to deep platter; sprinkle with bacon.

EACH SERVING: ABOUT 400 CALORIES | 52G PROTEIN | 20G CARBOHYDRATE | 13G TOTAL FAT (4G SATURATED) | 5G FIBER | 156MG CHOLESTEROL | 690MG SODIUM

CHICKEN TAGINE

This Moroccan stew features tender chicken thighs and butternut squash married with garlic, onion, and rich spices in the gentle heat of the slow cooker. (See page 10 for photo.)

ACTIVE TIME: 20 MINUTES · **TOTAL TIME:** 8 HOURS
MAKES: 6 MAIN-DISH SERVINGS

- 1 MEDIUM (1½-POUND) BUTTERNUT SQUASH, PEELED AND CUT INTO 2-INCH CHUNKS
- 2 MEDIUM TOMATOES, COARSELY CHOPPED
- 1 MEDIUM ONION, CHOPPED
- 2 CLOVES GARLIC, CRUSHED WITH PRESS
- 1 CAN (15- TO 19-OUNCE) GARBANZO BEANS, RINSED AND DRAINED
- 1 CUP CHICKEN BROTH

- ⅓ CUP RAISINS
- 2 TEASPOONS GROUND CORIANDER
- 2 TEASPOONS GROUND CUMIN
- ½ TEASPOON GROUND CINNAMON
- ½ TEASPOON SALT
- ¼ TEASPOON PEPPER
- 3 POUNDS BONE-IN SKINLESS CHICKEN THIGHS
- 1 BOX (10 OUNCES) PLAIN COUSCOUS
- ½ CUP PITTED GREEN OLIVES

1 In 6-quart slow cooker, combine squash, tomatoes, onion, garlic, beans, broth, and raisins. In cup, combine coriander, cumin, cinnamon, salt, and ground black pepper. Rub spice mixture all over chicken thighs; place chicken on top of vegetable mixture. Cover slow cooker with lid and cook as manufacturer directs, on low setting 8 hours or on high setting 4 hours.
2 About 10 minutes before serving, prepare couscous as label directs.
3 To serve, fluff couscous with fork. Stir olives into chicken mixture. Serve chicken mixture over couscous.

EACH SERVING: ABOUT 545 CALORIES | 39G PROTEIN | 80G CARBOHYDRATE | 9G TOTAL FAT (2G SATURATED) | 11G FIBER | 107MG CHOLESTEROL | 855MG SODIUM

RED-COOKED TURKEY THIGHS WITH LEEKS

Slow cookers make the most of economical cuts of meat. Here turkey thighs are cooked until succulent in a deeply flavorful sauce.

ACTIVE TIME: 20 MINUTES · **TOTAL TIME:** 8 HOURS
MAKES: 6 MAIN-DISH SERVINGS

4 LARGE LEEKS (ABOUT 2 POUNDS)

½ CUP DRY SHERRY

⅓ CUP SOY SAUCE

¼ CUP PACKED BROWN SUGAR

2 TABLESPOONS MINCED PEELED FRESH GINGER

1 TEASPOON CHINESE FIVE-SPICE POWDER

3 SMALL TURKEY THIGHS (ABOUT 1 POUND EACH), SKIN REMOVED

3 GARLIC CLOVES, CRUSHED WITH PRESS

3 CARROTS (8 OUNCES), PEELED AND CUT INTO ½-INCH SLICES

1 Cut off root and dark-green tops from leeks. Discard tough outer leaves. Cut each leek lengthwise in half then crosswise in half. Rinse leeks in large bowl of cold water, swishing to remove sand. Transfer leeks to colander, leaving sand in bowl.

2 In 4½- to 6-quart slow cooker, combine sherry, soy sauce, sugar, ginger, and five-spice powder. Add leeks, turkey, garlic, and carrots, and toss to coat with soy mixture. Cover slow cooker with lid and cook as manufacturer directs, on low setting 8 to 10 hours and high setting 4 to 5 hours.

3 Transfer turkey and vegetables to deep platter. Skim and discard fat from cooking liquid. Spoon cooking liquid over turkey and vegetables.

EACH SERVING: ABOUT 355 CALORIES | 41G PROTEIN | 24G CARBOHYDRATE | 10G TOTAL FAT (3G SATURATED) | 2G FIBER | 112 MG CHOLESTEROL | 1,005 MG SODIUM

INDIAN CAULIFLOWER CURRY STEW

This healthy vegetarian entrée is as cheap as can be—and a cinch to make in a slow cooker.

ACTIVE TIME: 25 MINUTES · **TOTAL TIME:** 50 MINUTES
MAKES: 8 MAIN-DISH SERVINGS

1   TABLESPOON OLIVE OIL

3   MEDIUM CARROTS, CHOPPED

1   MEDIUM ONION, CHOPPED

1½ CUPS BROWN RICE

1   TABLESPOON CURRY POWDER

¾   TEASPOON SALT

2½ CUPS VEGETABLE BROTH

1   MEDIUM HEAD CAULIFLOWER
    (2 POUNDS), CUT INTO SMALL
    FLORETS (4½ CUPS)

2   CANS (15 TO 19 OUNCES EACH)
    GARBANZO BEANS, RINSED AND
    DRAINED

½   CUP LOOSELY PACKED FRESH
    CILANTRO LEAVES, CHOPPED

⅓   CUP PLAIN LOW-FAT YOGURT PLUS
    ADDITIONAL FOR SERVING

1   In 6-quart Dutch oven, heat oil over medium-high heat until hot. Add carrots and onion, and cook 10 to 12 minutes or until vegetables are lightly browned and tender, stirring frequently.

2   Meanwhile, prepare rice as label directs; keep warm.

3   Stir ginger, curry, and salt into carrot mixture; cook 3 minutes, stirring constantly. Add broth; cover and heat to boiling over high heat. Stir in cauliflower and garbanzo beans; cover and cook over medium heat 15 to 20 minutes longer, gently stirring every 5 minutes until cauliflower is tender.

4   To serve, stir chopped cilantro and ¼ cup yogurt into cauliflower stew. Spoon rice into serving bowls; top with stew. Serve with additional yogurt to dollop on top, if you like. Makes about 8 cups.

EACH SERVING: ABOUT 360 CALORIES | 12G PROTEIN | 68G CARBOHYDRATE | 5G TOTAL FAT (1G SATURATED) | 10G FIBER | 1MG CHOLESTEROL | 650MG SODIUM

STRATEGY 2:
ONE DISH, MANY MEALS

As any budget-conscious cook knows, to trim the fat off your weekly grocery bill you must take full advantage of your leftovers. This sound sensible enough, and yet, your resolve may falter when your family whines about eating casserole AGAIN. Here you'll find an assortment of leftover-friendly recipes that can be easily turned into three and sometimes *four* meals apiece: one dish, many meals—what could be easier or more affordable than that? Whether you're roasting a chicken or turkey, pot roast or ham, or simply simmering a big pot of beans, we'll show you how to turn the fruits of your labor into a trio of satisfying meals.

Making mealtime easier for you is one of our key goals. See Fast Ways to Make Over Leftovers (page 30) for more transformative ideas. Of course, maximizing leftovers and minimizing your grocery bill may also mean relying on yourself to prepare some of the basics. Don't be daunted; just follow our simple step-by-step instructions for chicken broth (page 108), turkey broth (page 53), and home-cooked beans (page 31). You may never go back to canned again.

Counterclockwise from top: Roast Turkey with Pears and Onions; Dilly Turkey and Vegetables with Biscuits; Turkey Vegetable Soup (pages 48 to 53)

① LEMON-PEPPER ROAST CHICKEN

Why spring for supermarket rotisserie chicken when you can roast your own three-pounder in an hour for half the price? This Lemon-Pepper Roast Chicken is simply seasoned but delicious. Roast two and you'll have the basis for two more hearty dinners: Spicy Chicken Quesadillas and Chicken and Sausage Jambalaya.

ACTIVE TIME: 10 MINUTES · **TOTAL TIME:** 1 HOUR 10 MINUTES

MAKES: 4 MAIN-DISH SERVINGS PLUS ENOUGH LEFTOVERS FOR FOLLOWING RECIPES

2	WHOLE CHICKEN (3½ POUNDS EACH)	½	TEASPOON GROUND BLACK PEPPER
2	TABLESPOONS OLIVE OIL	1½	TEASPOONS SALT
4	TEASPOONS GRATED LEMON PEEL	1	CUP WATER

1 Preheat oven to 450°F. Remove bags with giblets and neck from chicken cavities; discard or reserve for another use.

2 In cup, mix oil, lemon peel, and pepper. With fingertips, gently separate skin from meat on chicken breasts. Rub lemon-pepper mixture on meat under skin. Tie legs together with string. Rub chickens all over with salt.

3 Place chickens, breasts side up, on rack in large roasting pan (12½" by 16½"). Pour ½ cup water into roasting pan. Roast chickens 1 hour or until juices run clear when thickest part of thighs is pierced with tip of knife and temperature on meat thermometer inserted into thickest part of thighs reaches 175°F.

4 When chickens are done, lift from roasting pan and tilt slightly to allow juices inside cavity to run into pan. Place chicken on platter. Let chickens stand 10 minutes to allow juices to set for easier carving.

5 Remove rack from roasting pan. Skim and discard fat from pan juices. Add remaining ½ cup water to pan juices; cook 1 minute on medium, stirring constantly. Serve one chicken with pan juices. Let other chicken cool 30 minutes; refrigerate in an airtight container for up to 3 days.

EACH SERVING: ABOUT 425 CALORIES | 42G PROTEIN | 0G CARBOHYDRATE | 27G TOTAL FAT (7G SATURATED) | 0G FIBER | 134MG CHOLESTEROL | 565MG SODIUM

② SPICY CHICKEN QUESADILLAS

Leftover Lemon-Pepper Roast Chicken is put to good use in these quick and easy quesadillas. Look for salsa verde, a tangy, mild salsa made from tomatillos rather than tomatoes, in your local supermarket.

ACTIVE TIME: 25 MINUTES · **TOTAL TIME:** 35 MINUTES

MAKES 4 MAIN-DISH SERVINGS

---

2   GREEN ONIONS

2   CUPS SHREDDED, SKINLESS, BONELESS ROASTED CHICKEN BREAST (PAGE 26)

6   OUNCES MONTEREY JACK CHEESE, SHREDDED (1½ CUPS)

1   PICKLED JALAPEÑO CHILE, FINELY CHOPPED

¼   CUP LOOSELY PACKED FRESH CILANTRO LEAVES, CHOPPED (OPTIONAL)

4   BURRITO-SIZE (10-INCH) FLOUR TORTILLAS

¼   CUP SALSA VERDE

½   CUP REDUCED-FAT SOUR CREAM

1 Thinly slice green onions; reserve 2 tablespoons dark green tops for garnish.

2 Heat 12-inch skillet over medium heat until hot. Place 1 tortilla in skillet. Sprinkle with one-half of chicken, cheese, jalapeño, cilantro, if using, and green onion; top with second tortilla, pressing lightly. Cook quesadilla about 2 minutes or until lightly toasted. Carefully turn quesadilla and cook 1 to 2 minutes longer or until cheese melts. Repeat with remaining tortillas and ingredients.

3 Cut quesadillas into wedges; place on large dinner plates and serve with salsa verde and sour cream. Sprinkle with reserved green onions.

EACH SERVING: ABOUT 560 CALORIES | 39G PROTEIN | 41G CARBOHYDRATE | 25G TOTAL FAT (12G SATURATED) | 2G FIBER | 108MG CHOLESTEROL | 1,130MG SODIUM

③ CHICKEN AND SAUSAGE JAMBALAYA

Our Jambalaya, a traditional Creole rice dish, is a brilliant use of leftover roasted chicken—we used Lemon-Pepper Roast Chicken—smoked sausage, and vegetables cooked in a zesty, tomato-enhanced chicken broth.

ACTIVE TIME: 35 MINUTES · **TOTAL TIME:** 1 HOUR

MAKES 4 MAIN-DISH SERVINGS

- 4 OUNCES KIELBASA (SMOKED POLISH SAUSAGE) OR HOT SMOKED SAUSAGE LINKS, THINLY SLICED
- 1 TEASPOON VEGETABLE OIL
- 2 WHOLE ROASTED CHICKEN LEGS, SKIN AND BONES REMOVED, CUT INTO 1-INCH CHUNKS (PAGE 26)
- 3 CLOVES GARLIC, CRUSHED WITH PRESS
- 2 LARGE CELERY STALKS, SLICED
- 1 MEDIUM GREEN AND/OR YELLOW PEPPERS, CUT INTO ½-INCH PIECES
- 1 MEDIUM ONION, CHOPPED
- 1½ CUPS (LONG-GRAIN) WHITE RICE
- ½ TEASPOON PAPRIKA
- ⅜ TEASPOON DRIED OREGANO
- ¼ TEASPOON DRIED THYME
- ½ TEASPOON SALT
- ¾ CUP PLUS 2 TABLESPOONS CHICKEN BROTH (PAGE 108)
- 1 CUP DICED TOMATOES
- ½ CUP WATER
- ¼ TEASPOON HOT PEPPER SAUCE

1 Preheat oven to 425°F.

2 In deep 12-inch skillet with oven-safe handle and lid (or with handle and lid handle wrapped in double thickness of foil for baking in oven later), cook kielbasa over medium-high heat 2 to 3 minutes or until browned, stirring occasionally. With slotted spoon, transfer kielbasa to medium bowl; add chicken legs.

3 Reduce heat to medium, and add oil to skillet. Stir in garlic, celery, peppers, and onions; cover and cook 12 to 15 minutes or until vegetables are tender, stirring occasionally. Add rice, paprika, oregano, thyme, and salt, and cook 1 minute, stirring.

4 Return chicken and kielbasa to skillet. Add broth, tomatoes with their juice, water, and hot pepper sauce; heat to boiling over high heat.

5 Place skillet in oven and bake jambalaya, uncovered, 15 minutes. Remove skillet from oven and stir. Cover and bake 10 minutes longer or until rice is tender. Remove skillet from oven; let stand, covered, 10 minutes.

EACH SERVING: ABOUT 490 CALORIES | 24G PROTEIN | 72G CARBOHYDRATE | 11G TOTAL FAT (3G SATURATED) | 4G FIBER | 64MG CHOLESTEROL | 1,290MG SODIUM

FAST WAYS TO MAKE OVER LEFTOVERS

These ingredients give suppers a second act—and stretch your dollars even further.

- **Tortillas:** The possibilities for these Latin staples are endless. Roll up a combo of yesterday's roasted chicken, a scoop of cooked rice, and some canned black beans to make burritos; for beef fajitas, cut up leftover pot roast and mix it with sautéed peppers and onions. And for everything-but-the-kitchen-sink nachos, make homemade chips by microwaving flour or corn tortillas. Cut each tortilla into 6 pieces. Arrange in single layer between dry paper towels; cook on High 1 minute.

- **Ready-made Pizza Crusts:** Keep 'em in your freezer, and create original pizzas with everything from roast turkey to extra ground beef from that family-size package.

- **Broth:** Soup comes together in a flash with chicken or vegetable broth plus last night's rice pilaf and frozen veggies. Or throw together a quick "risotto" using 1 cup raw rice, 4 cups broth, and leftover vegetables.

- **Eggs:** These amazingly versatile protein packets can turn any entrée extras into a dazzling frittata, omelet, or quiche. Scramble a few with some cooked rice and second-act shrimp, and you don't have to spring for Chinese takeout.

- **Lettuce:** Transform yesterday's chicken into a tasty salad with a head of romaine, sliced apple, some toasted nuts, and a drizzle of your favorite dressing.

- **Canned Tomatoes:** Nothing comes in more handy at mealtime. Think red rice or gumbo, or revamp day-old pasta with a quick tomato sauce.

- **Ramen Noodles:** Perfect for a busy weeknight, these squares of noodles cook up in mere minutes, and you can use as much or as little of the flavoring packet as you like. For a savory soup, add thin slices of leftover cooked pork along with a handful each of snow peas and shredded carrot. Or cook the noodles separately, then sauté with the veggies for a simple lo mein.

HOME-COOKED BEANS

There's no better budget stretcher than beans. Follow our basic recipe, and you're well on your way to creating three more deliciously affordable meals. Feel free to swap in pinto beans, cannellini beans, black beans—whatever dried beans you have in your pantry.

ACTIVE TIME: 10 MINUTES · **TOTAL TIME:** 1 HOUR PLUS SOAKING OVERNIGHT

MAKES: 10 TO 12 CUPS BEANS, ENOUGH TO MAKE FOLLOWING RECIPES

---

2   BAGS (16 OUNCES EACH) DRIED RED KIDNEY BEANS

1   LARGE ONION, CUT IN QUARTERS

2   CLOVES GARLIC, CRUSHED WITH GARLIC PRESS

2   SPRIG PARSLEY

2   BAY LEAF

1   In colander, rinse beans well with cold water; discard any stones or shriveled beans. In 8-quart saucepot, place beans and enough *water* to cover by 2 inches.

2   Drain beans and return to saucepot. Add onion, garlic, parsley, bay leaf, and 6 *cups water*; heat to boiling on high. Reduce heat to medium-low; partially cover and simmer 45 to 60 minutes or until beans are tender, stirring occasionally. (Reserve 1½ *cups bean cooking liquid* if making Cajun Red Beans and Rice, page 32.) Drain beans. Discard parsley and bay leaf. If not using beans right away, cover and refrigerate up to 5 days, or pack in airtight containers and freeze up to 6 months.

EACH SERVING: ABOUT 260 CALORIES | 17G PROTEIN | 48G CARBOHYDRATE | 1G TOTAL FAT (1G SATURATED) | 12G FIBER | 0MG CHOLESTEROL | 10MG SODIUM

② CAJUN RED BEANS AND RICE

This classic New Orleans beans and rice dish garners flavor from celery, bacon, and dried herbs. Leftover baked ham (see page 37) makes a great substitute for bacon if you have it on hand.

ACTIVE TIME: 10 MINUTES · **TOTAL TIME:** 30 MINUTES PLUS PREPARING BEANS
MAKES: 4 MAIN-DISH SERVINGS

- 1 CUP REGULAR LONG-GRAIN WHITE RICE
- 2 SLICES BACON, CUT INTO ½-INCH PIECES
- 1 SMALL ONION, CHOPPED
- 2 STALKS CELERY, SLICED
- 1 GREEN PEPPER, CHOPPED

- 2 CLOVES GARLIC, FINELY CHOPPED
- 2 TEASPOONS CAJUN SEASONING
- ½ TEASPOON DRIED THYME
- ¼ TEASPOON SALT
- 2½ CUPS HOME-COOKED BEANS (PAGE 31) PLUS 1½ CUPS BEAN COOKING WATER
- ¼ TEASPOON CAYENNE PEPPER SAUCE

1   Prepare rice as label directs.
2   Meanwhile, in 12-inch nonstick skillet, cook bacon on medium heat until browned. With slotted spoon, transfer bacon to paper towels to drain.
3   To bacon fat in skillet, add onion, celery, green pepper, garlic, Cajun seasoning, thyme, and salt. Cook 10 to 12 minutes or until vegetables are tender, stirring occasionally. Stir in beans and reserved bean cooking water, bacon, and cayenne pepper sauce. Cook 3 to 5 minutes longer to blend flavors.
4   Serve bean mixture over rice.

EACH SERVING: ABOUT 505 CALORIES | 29G PROTEIN | 82G CARBOHYDRATE | 8G TOTAL FAT (2G SATURATED) | 13G FIBER | 25MG CHOLESTEROL | 990MG SODIUM

WALLET-FRIENDLY TIPS: BEANS

Beans can't be beat when it comes to a low-cost source of good nutrition. They are packed with protein and insoluable and soluable fiber, and they're high in saponin, a cancer-fighting plant compound. You can enjoy a can of beans for about one-third of the cost of ground beef. Incorporate beans into salads (warm or cold), stews, casseroles, and veggie burgers.

Want even more bang for your buck? Buy dried beans, lentils, and split peas instead of canned—and make homemade beans for less than one-third of the cost. Divide them into 1½ cup portions (the equivalent of a 15.5-ounce can), pack in airtight containers, and freeze for up to 6 months. For an easy, versatile recipe, see Home-Cooked Beans, page 31.

③ VEGGIE BEAN BURGERS

Serve this vegetarian main dish with a side of shredded carrots tossed with a squeeze of lime and a sprinkling of black pepper.

ACTIVE TIME: 10 MINUTES · **TOTAL TIME:** 20 MINUTES PLUS PREPARING BEANS
MAKES: 4 MAIN-DISH SERVINGS

2 CUPS HOME-COOKED BEANS (PAGE 31)

2 TABLESPOONS LIGHT MAYONNAISE

⅓ CUP LOOSELY PACKED FRESH CILANTRO LEAVES

1 TABLESPOON PLAIN DRIED BREAD CRUMBS

1 TEASPOON GROUND CUMIN

1 TEASPOON CAYENNE PEPPER SAUCE

¼ TEASPOON SALT

NONSTICK COOKING SPRAY

1 TABLESPOON OLIVE OIL

4 LETTUCE LEAVES

1 LARGE TOMATO, CUT INTO 4 SLICES

4 HAMBURGER BUNS, SPLIT AND TOASTED

1 In large bowl, with potato masher or fork, mash beans with mayonnaise until almost smooth (some lumps of beans should remain). Stir in cilantro leaves, bread crumbs, ground cumin, hot pepper sauce, and salt until well combined. Divide bean mixture in quarters; with lightly floured hands, shape each into a 3-inch round patty. Lightly spray both sides of each patty with nonstick cooking spray.

2 In 12-inch nonstick skillet, heat olive oil on medium 1 minute. Add bean patties, and cook about 10 minutes or until lightly browned on both sides and heated through.

3 Arrange lettuce and tomato slices on bottoms of buns; top with patties and bun tops.

EACH BURGER: ABOUT 345 CALORIES | 14G PROTEIN | 52G CARBOHYDRATE | 9G TOTAL FAT (2G SATURATED) | 9G FIBER | 13MG CHOLESTEROL | 520MG SODIUM

④ SOUTH-OF-THE-BORDER VEGETABLE HASH

A savory combination of classic hash ingredients (without the meat) gets a new flavor twist from kidney beans, cilantro, and fresh lime.

ACTIVE TIME: 20 MINUTES · **TOTAL TIME:** 50 MINUTES

MAKES: 4 MAIN-DISH SERVINGS

---

3   LARGE YUKON GOLD POTATOES (ABOUT 1½ POUNDS), CUT INTO ¾-INCH CHUNKS

2   TABLESPOONS OLIVE OIL

1   LARGE ONION, CUT INTO ¼-INCH DICE

1   MEDIUM GREEN OR RED PEPPER, CUT INTO ¼-INCH-WIDE STRIPS

3   GARLIC CLOVES, CRUSHED WITH GARLIC PRESS

2   TEASPOONS GROUND CUMIN

¾   TEASPOON SALT

2   CUPS HOME-COOKED BEANS (PAGE 31)

2   TABLESPOONS CHOPPED FRESH CILANTRO LEAVES

ACCOMPANIMENTS: PLAIN YOGURT, LIME WEDGES, SALSA, AND TOASTED CORN TORTILLAS (OPTIONAL)

1   In 3-quart saucepan, place potato chunks and enough *water* to cover; heat to boiling over high heat. Reduce heat to low; cover and simmer about 5 minutes or until potatoes are almost tender; drain well.

2   Meanwhile, in nonstick 12-inch skillet, heat oil over medium-high heat until hot. Add onion, pepper, garlic, cumin, and salt, and cook 10 minutes. Add drained potatoes, and cook 5 minutes longer or until vegetables are lightly browned. Stir in beans, and cook 2 minutes longer or until heated through. Sprinkle with chopped cilantro.

3   Serve vegetable hash with yogurt, lime wedges, salsa, and corn tortillas, if you like.

EACH SERVING: ABOUT 360 CALORIES | 12G PROTEIN | 63G CARBOHYDRATE | 8G TOTAL FAT (1G SATURATED) | 13G FIBER | 0MG CHOLESTEROL | 625MG SODIUM

(1) APRICOT-MUSTARD GLAZED HAM

This succulent ham is only the beginning. Use the leftovers to make three satisfying suppers: ham steak with cheese grits, an impressive-looking soufflé, and a warming split pea soup.

ACTIVE TIME: 15 MINUTES · **TOTAL TIME:** 1 HOUR 45 MINUTES

MAKES: 4 MAIN-DISH SERVINGS PLUS ENOUGH LEFTOVERS FOR FOLLOWING RECIPES

- 1 FULLY-COOKED, SMOKED, BONE-IN SHANK-HALF HAM (7 POUNDS)
- ⅓ CUP APRICOT PRESERVES
- 1 TABLESPOON DIJON MUSTARD

1 Preheat oven to 325°F. If necessary, with sharp knife, remove skin and trim fat from ham, leaving about 1¼-inch-thick layer of fat. Place ham in small (14" by 10") roasting pan; bake 1 hour.

2 In small bowl, stir apricot preserves and mustard until blended.

3 Remove ham from oven; brush with glaze. Return to oven and bake 25 to 30 minutes longer or until meat thermometer inserted in thickest part of ham (not touching bone) reaches 130°F. Internal temperature of ham will rise 5 to 10°F upon standing.

4 Transfer ham to warm platter and let stand 15 minutes to set juices before slicing. Pack leftover ham in an airtight container. (Reserve ham bone if making Split Pea Soup with Ham, page 42.) Refrigerate for up to 3 days.

EACH SERVING: ABOUT 194 CALORIES | 22G PROTEIN | 4G CARBOHYDRATE | 9G TOTAL FAT (3G SATURATED) | 0G FIBER | 58MG CHOLESTEROL | 1,513MG SODIUM

② HAM STEAK WITH CREAMY CHEESE GRITS

What's not to like about this comforting fare that capitalizes on leftover ham?

TOTAL TIME: 20 MINUTES

MAKES: 4 MAIN-DISH SERVINGS

1¼ CUPS WHOLE MILK

1   CAN (14 TO 14½ OUNCES) CHICKEN OR VEGETABLE BROTH (1¾ CUPS)

¼   TEASPOON GROUND RED PEPPER (CAYENNE)

¼   TEASPOON DRIED THYME

¾   CUP QUICK GRITS

1   CUP SHREDDED CHEDDAR CHEESE

4   SLICES BAKED HAM (1¼ POUNDS), ½-INCH THICK (PAGE 37)

2   TABLESPOONS LIGHT BROWN SUGAR

GREEN ONIONS FOR GARNISH (OPTIONAL)

1   In 2-quart saucepan, combine milk, broth, pepper, and thyme; heat to boiling over high heat. Slowly whisk grits into liquid. Reduce heat to low; cover and simmer 5 to 7 minutes or until mixture thickens, stirring occasionally. Remove saucepan from heat and stir in Cheddar.

2   While grits are cooking, prepare ham: Heat nonstick 12-inch skillet over medium-high heat until hot. Pat ham dry with paper towels. Coat both sides of ham with sugar; add to skillet. Cook ham 5 minutes or until heated through and generously glazed, turning once. To serve, arrange ham on platter with pan juices and grits. Garnish with green onions, if you like.

EACH SERVING: ABOUT 560 CALORIES | 42G PROTEIN | 40G CARBOHYDRATE | 25G TOTAL FAT (12G SATURATED) | 0.5G FIBER | 115MG CHOLESTEROL | 2,625MG SODIUM

③ HAM AND PEPPER JACK SOUFFLÉ

Leftover ham and pepper Jack cheese partner up in this light and fluffy soufflé. For teriffic ideas to complete the meal, see Side Salad in a Snap, page 43.

ACTIVE TIME: 20 MINUTES · **TOTAL TIME:** 1 HOUR 10 MINUTES
MAKES: 6 MAIN-DISH SERVINGS

- 4 TABLESPOONS BUTTER OR MARGARINE
- ¼ CUP ALL-PURPOSE FLOUR
- 1½ CUPS REDUCED-FAT (2%) MILK, WARMED
- 6 OUNCES PEPPER JACK CHEESE, SHREDDED (2 CUPS)

- 4 LARGE EGGS, SEPARATED
- 1 LARGE EGG WHITE
- 1 CUP CHOPPED HAM (PAGE 37)
- 1 CAN (4½-OUNCE) CHOPPED MILD GREEN CHILES, DRAINED

1 Preheat oven to 325°F. Grease 2-quart soufflé dish.

2 In heavy 2-quart saucepan, melt butter on low. Add flour and cook 1 minute, stirring. With wire whisk, gradually mix in milk. Cook on medium until sauce thickens and boils, stirring constantly. Reduce heat to low and simmer 3 minutes, stirring frequently. Stir in pepper Jack and cook just until cheese melts and sauce is smooth, stirring. Remove saucepan from heat.

3 In medium bowl, with whisk, lightly beat egg yolks; gradually whisk in hot cheese sauce. Stir in ham and green chiles.

4 In large bowl, with mixer on high speed, beat 5 egg whites until stiff peaks form when beaters are lifted. With rubber spatula, gently fold one-third of beaten egg whites into cheese mixture. Fold in remaining whites just until blended.

5 Pour mixture into prepared soufflé dish. Bake about 50 minutes or until soufflé is puffed and golden-brown and knife inserted 1 inch from edge comes out clean. Serve immediately.

EACH SERVING: ABOUT 315 CALORIES | 17G PROTEIN | 10G CARBOHYDRATE | 22G TOTAL FAT (9G SATURATED) | 0.5G FIBER | 187MG CHOLESTEROL | 652MG SODIUM

④ SPLIT PEA SOUP WITH HAM

This hearty old-fashioned favorite is a perfect pick-me up on a cold blustery day.

ACTIVE TIME: 10 MINUTES · **TOTAL TIME:** 45 MINUTES
MAKES: 6 MAIN-DISH SERVINGS

- 2 TABLESPOONS VEGETABLE OIL
- 2 WHITE TURNIPS (6 OUNCES EACH), PEELED AND CHOPPED (OPTIONAL)
- 2 CARROTS, PEELED AND FINELY CHOPPED
- 2 STALKS CELERY, FINELY CHOPPED
- 1 MEDIUM ONION, FINELY CHOPPED
- 1 PACKAGE (16 OUNCES) DRY SPLIT PEAS, RINSED AND PICKED THROUGH
- 1 HAM BONE (1½ POUNDS), PLUS 2 CUPS CHOPPED HAM (PAGE 37)
- 8 CUPS WATER
- 1 BAY LEAF
- 1 TEASPOON SALT
- ¼ TEASPOON GROUND ALLSPICE

1 In 5-quart Dutch oven, heat oil over medium-high heat. Add turnips, if using, carrots, celery, and onion; cook, stirring frequently, until carrots are tender-crisp, about 10 minutes. Add split peas, ham bone, water, bay leaf, salt, and allspice; heat to boiling over high heat. Reduce heat; cover and simmer 45 minutes.

2 Discard bay leaf. Remove bone. Add meat to soup, and heat through.

EACH SERVING: ABOUT 365 CALORIES | 26G PROTEIN | 46G CARBOHYDRATE | 9G TOTAL FAT (2G SATURATED) | 17G FIBER | 26MG CHOLESTEROL | 1,086MG SODIUM

SIDE SALAD IN A SNAP

Pair a quick salad with one of our pasta dishes and dinner is served! It all starts with a basic vinaigrette: In a small bowl, whisk together 3 tablespoons vinegar, ½ teaspoon Dijon mustard, and a pinch of salt and pepper, then slowly drizzle in ¼ cup olive oil, whisking until the mixture emulsifies. Change the flavor by using a different vinegar, such as balsamic, sherry, or tarragon, or experiment with your own favorite flavors.

- **Baby Romaine with Fennel and Citrus:** Toss together 8 cups baby romaine; 1 cup thinly sliced fennel; 1 cup jarred citrus segments; ½ cup rinsed and drained chickpeas; and 6 sliced radishes. Dressing tip: Use lemon juice or a combination of lemon and lime juice instead of vinegar.

- **Greek Salad with Feta and Olives:** Toss together 8 cups mixed baby greens; 1 cup grape tomatoes; 1 seedless cucumber, cut into ½-inch chunks; and 1½ cup pitted kalamata olives. Top with ¼ cup crumbled goat or feta cheese. Dressing tip: Use tarragon or white wine vinegar.

- **Carrot Coleslaw with Dried Cherries and Almonds:** Toss together 4 cups shredded carrots; 1 large red pepper, cut into ¼-inch-wide strips; ½ cup dried cherries; and ½ cup toasted slivered almonds. Dressing tip: Use seasoned rice vinegar and add a teaspoon of toasted sesame oil.

- **Apple Coleslaw with Golden Raisins with Pecans:** Toss together one 16-ounce bag coleslaw mix; 1 Granny Smith apple, cored and cut into ½-inch chunks; ½ cup golden raisins; and ½ cup chopped pecans. Dressing tip: Whisk 1 tablespoon light mayonnaise into basic vinaigrette.

- **Spinach and Endive with Pears and Walnuts:** Toss together 10 cups baby spinach; 2 heads Belgian endive, sliced; 1 Bosc pear, cored and cut into thin slices; and ½ cup toasted walnut pieces. Dressing tip: Use raspberry vinegar.

① POT ROAST WITH FALL VEGETABLES

Our pot roast makes enough for three meals. Serve one roast with the vegetables and gravy, then use the leftovers to make hearty open-faced sandwiches or easy spaghetti bolognese.

ACTIVE TIME: 30 MINUTES · TOTAL TIME: 3 HOURS 15 MINUTES

MAKES: 4-MAIN DISH SERVINGS PLUS ENOUGH LEFTOVERS FOR FOLLOWING RECIPES

---

1   TEASPOON DRIED THYME

3   TEASPOONS SALT

1   TEASPOON COARSELY GROUND BLACK PEPPER

2   BONELESS BEEF CHUCK OR BOTTOM ROUND ROASTS (3½ TO 4 POUNDS EACH), TRIMMED OF FAT

2   MEDIUM ONIONS (1 POUND), CHOPPED

2   CLOVES GARLIC, CRUSHED WITH PRESS

1   CAN (14- TO 14½ OUNCES) BEEF BROTH

2   CUPS WATER

2   TEASPOONS WORCESTERSHIRE SAUCE

1   BAY LEAF

2   POUNDS ALL-PURPOSE POTATOES (6 MEDIUM), UNPEELED AND CUT INTO 1-INCH CHUNKS

6   CARROTS (1 POUND), CUT INTO 1-INCH CHUNKS

2   POUNDS GREEN BEANS, TRIMMED AND EACH CUT IN HALF

---

1   Preheat oven to 350°F. In cup, combine thyme, salt, and pepper; use rub all over roasts.

2   In 12-quart Dutch oven, heat oil over medium-high heat until hot. Add roasts and cook about 10 minutes or until well browned on all sides. Transfer roasts to plate. Reduce heat to medium. Add onions and garlic to Dutch oven, and cook 8 minutes or until lightly browned, stirring occasionally. Stir in broth, water, Worcestershire, and bay leaf; heat to boiling over high heat. Return roasts to Dutch oven; cover and place in oven. Cook 2 hours.

3   After roasts have cooked 2 hours, stir in potatoes and carrots; cover and cook in oven 30 minutes longer. Place green beans on top of roasts and vegetables in Dutch oven; cover and cook in oven 15 minutes longer or until meat and all vegetables are tender.

4   Place 1 roast on warm large platter; discard bay leaf. Place other roast in an airtight container and refrigerate for up to 3 days. Transfer 1 cup each vegetables and liquid from Dutch oven to food processor with knife blade attached. Spoon remaining vegetables around roast; cover to keep warm. Discard fat from liquid in Dutch oven.

5 Pulse vegetable mixture in food processor until pureed. Add pureed vegetables to liquid remaining in Dutch oven to make gravy; heat over medium until hot. Makes 3⅔ cups gravy. Serve pot roast and vegetables with gravy.

EACH SERVING: ABOUT 454 CALORIES | 47G PROTEIN | 37G CARBOHYDRATE | 13G TOTAL FAT (4G SATURATED) | 8G FIBER | 83MG CHOLESTEROL | 766MG SODIUM

② OPEN-FACE BRISKET SANDWICHES

A refreshing jicama salad rounds out this quick and easy meal.

ACTIVE TIME: 10 MINUTES · **TOTAL TIME:** 15 MINUTES
MAKES: 4 MAIN-DISH SERVINGS

JICAMA SALAD

- 1 SMALL JICAMA (8 OUNCES), PEELED AND DICED
- 1 LARGE RED PEPPER (8 TO 10 OUNCES), CHOPPED
- 1 CUP FROZEN CORN KERNELS, THAWED
- 1 SMALL JALAPEÑO CHILE, STEMMED, SEEDED, AND FINELY CHOPPED
- ¼ CUP CILANTRO LEAVES, CHOPPED
- 2 TABLESPOONS FRESH LIME JUICE
- 1 TEASPOON SUGAR
- ½ TEASPOON SALT
- ¼ TEASPOON FRESHLY GROUND BLACK PEPPER

BRISKET SANDWICHES

NONSTICK COOKING SPRAY

- 1 PACKAGE (16 OUNCES) MUSHROOMS, TRIMMED AND SLICED
- ¼ CUP CHILI SAUCE
- 1 TABLESPOON CHILI POWDER
- 2 TABLESPOONS RED WINE VINEGAR
- 1 TEASPOON SUGAR
- ¼ CUP WATER
- 1 TEASPOON SALT
- 8 THIN SLICES POT ROAST (PAGE 44)
- 2 FRENCH-BREAD ROLLS (6 INCHES LONG, 4 OUNCES EACH)
- 2 MEDIUM TOMATOES (1 POUND)
- 1 HEAD BOSTON LETTUCE, TORN INTO 4 PIECES

1 In large bowl, place jicama, pepper, corn jalapeño, cilantro, lime juice, sugar, salt, and pepper. Stir until well combined, cover, and refrigerate.

2 Spray 12-inch skillet with nonstick cooking spray. Heat skillet over medium-high heat, and cook mushrooms 10 to 12 minutes until golden, stirring frequently. Set mushrooms aside in large bowl.

3 In same skillet, combine chili sauce, chili powder, red wine vinegar, sugar, water, and salt; over high heat, heat to boiling. Reduce heat to medium-low; boil 2 minutes. Add meat and mushrooms; toss to heat through.

4 Slice each French-bread roll horizontally in half. Slice tomatoes. Top cut sides of rolls with tomato slices, lettuce leaves, and beef mixture. Serve open-face sandwiches with jicama salad.

EACH SERVING: ABOUT 574 CALORIES | 54G PROTEIN | 63G CARBOHYDRATE | 12G TOTAL FAT (4G SATURATED) | 9G FIBER | 83MG CHOLESTEROL | 2,000MG SODIUM

③ QUICK SPAGHETTI BOLOGNESE

A simple but satisfying take on a Southern Italian classic.

ACTIVE TIME: 10 MINUTES · **TOTAL TIME:** 40 MINUTES

MAKES: 12 MAIN-DISH SERVINGS

- 2   TABLESPOONS OLIVE OIL
- 1   MEDIUM ONION (6 TO 8 OUNCES), CHOPPED
- 1   LARGE STALK CELERY, CHOPPED
- 1   LARGE CARROT, SHREDDED
- ¼   CUP TOMATO PASTE
- ½   CUP DRY RED WINE
- 1   CAN (28 OUNCES) WHOLE TOMATOES IN PUREE

- 1½ TEASPOONS SALT
- ¼   TEASPOON GROUND BLACK PEPPER
- 2   PACKAGES (16 OUNCES EACH) SPAGHETTI
- ½   CUP WHOLE MILK
- 2   CUPS FINELY CHOPPED POT ROAST MEAT (PAGE 44)

1 Heat oil in 5- or 6-quart Dutch oven over medium-high until hot. Add onion, celery, and carrot, and cook 10 minutes or until tender, stirring occasionally. Stir in tomato paste; cook 2 minutes.

2 Add red wine and cook 1 minute. Stir in tomatoes, salt, and pepper; heat to boiling, breaking up tomatoes with side of spoon. Reduce heat to medium-low; cover and simmer 15 minutes, stirring occasionally.

3 Stir milk and meat into sauce; cover and simmer 5 minutes. Toss sauce with spaghetti.

EACH SERVING: ABOUT 407 CALORIES │ 22G PROTEIN │ 63G CARBOHYDRATE │ 6G TOTAL FAT (2G SATURATED) │ 3G FIBER │ 22MG CHOLESTEROL │ 581MG SODIUM

① ROAST TURKEY WITH PEARS AND ONIONS

This traditional roasted turkey features juicy Bosc pears and fragrant dried thyme. You can make Dilly Turkey and Vegetables with Biscuits and Turkey Vegetable Soup for subsequent suppers, and still have enough leftover meat to enjoy turkey sandwiches at lunchtime.

ACTIVE TIME: 25 MINUTES · **TOTAL TIME:** 4 HOURS

MAKES: 4 MAIN-DISH SERVINGS WITH ENOUGH LEFTOVERS FOR FOLLOWING RECIPES

---

1 FRESH OR FROZEN (THAWED) TURKEY (14 POUNDS)

1½ TEASPOONS SALT

⅝ TEASPOON GROUND BLACK PEPPER

¾ TEASPOON DRIED THYME

2 LARGE RED ONIONS, EACH CUT INTO 8 WEDGES

3 RIPE BOSC PEARS, EACH CORED AND QUARTERED

1 TABLESPOON BUTTER OR MARGARINE, MELTED

½ CUP WATER

1   Preheat oven to 325°F.

2   Remove giblets and neck from turkey cavity; reserve for making Turkey Broth (page 53). Discard liver. Pat turkey dry with paper towels.

3   Place turkey, breast side up, on rack in large roasting pan (17" by 11½"). Rub outside of turkey all over with salt, ½ teaspoon pepper, and ½ teaspoon thyme. Place onions in pan around turkey; cover pan with a loose tent of foil; roast 2½ hours.

4   In bowl, toss pears with butter and remaining ⅛ teaspoon pepper and ¼ teaspoon thyme. Remove foil from turkey; add pears to pan around turkey. Roast turkey, uncovered, about 45 minutes longer. Turkey's done when temperature on meat thermometer inserted in thickest part of thigh, next to body (not touching bone), reaches 175 to 180°F and breast temperature reaches 165°F. (Internal temperature of turkey will rise 5 to 10°F upon standing.) If turkey is not done, remove pears and onions to platter; cover. Continue roasting turkey.

5   When turkey is done, lift from roasting pan and tilt slightly to allow juices inside cavity to run into pan. Place turkey on platter with onions and pears; let stand at least 15 minutes to allow juices to set for easier carving.

6 Remove rack from roasting pan. Add water to juices in pan. Place pan over 2 burners and cook on medium-high, stirring until browned bits are loosened from bottom of pan. Skim and discard fat. Makes about 1 cup pan juices. Carve enough turkey for 4 servings; serve along with pears, onions, and pan juices. Cover and refrigerate remaining turkey for up to 3 days. (Be sure to reserve turkey carcass, scraps, and neck if making Turkey Broth, page 53.)

EACH SERVING: ABOUT 300 CALORIES | 28G PROTEIN | 22G CARBOHYDRATE | 12G TOTAL FAT (3G SATURATED) | 4G FIBER | 71MG CHOLESTEROL | 315MG SODIUM

② DILLY TURKEY AND VEGETABLES WITH BISCUITS

Leftover roasted turkey and homemade turkey broth give this easy next-day dish a rich flavor.

ACTIVE TIME: 25 MINUTES · **TOTAL TIME:** 40 MINUTES

MAKES: 4 MAIN-DISH SERVINGS

- 2 TEASPOONS BAKING POWDER
- 1⅓ CUPS PLUS 2 TABLESPOONS ALL-PURPOSE FLOUR
- 1 TEASPOON SALT
- ½ TEASPOON COARSELY GROUND BLACK PEPPER
- 4 TABLESPOONS BUTTER OR MARGARINE
- 1 CUP REDUCED-FAT (2%) MILK
- 1 SMALL ONION, CHOPPED

- 3 MEDIUM CARROTS, CUT INTO ¼-INCH SLICES
- 2 STALKS CELERY, CUT INTO ¼-INCH SLICES
- 1½ CUPS TURKEY BROTH (PAGE 53)
- 1 CUP FROZEN PEAS
- 2 CUPS (½-INCH CHUNKS) SKINLESS COOKED LEFTOVER TURKEY (PAGE 48)
- ⅓ CUP LOOSELY PACKED FRESH DILL, CHOPPED (OPTIONAL)

1 Prepare shortcake biscuits: Preheat oven to 425°F. In medium bowl, combine baking powder, 1⅓ cups flour, ½ teaspoon salt, and ¼ teaspoon pepper. With pastry blender or 2 knives used scissors-fashion, cut in 3 tablespoons butter until mixture resembles coarse crumbs. Stir in ½ cup milk. With hand, knead mixture in bowl just until dough holds together. On ungreased cookie sheet, with lightly floured hands, pat dough into 6-inch square. With sharp knife, cut dough into 4 squares. Arrange squares 2 inches apart on cookie sheet. Bake biscuits 13 to 15 minutes.

2 Meanwhile, in 3-quart saucepan, melt remaining 1 tablespoon butter on medium heat. Add chopped onion and cook 5 minutes or until tender, stirring occasionally. Add carrots, celery, turkey broth, and remaining ½ teaspoon salt and ¼ teaspoon pepper; heat to boiling on high. Reduce heat to low and simmer 10 to 12 minutes or until all vegetables are tender.

3 In 1-cup liquid measuring cup, whisk remaining 2 tablespoons flour into remaining ½ cup milk. In thin, steady stream, pour milk mixture into hot turkey broth, whisking constantly. Heat to boiling; boil 1 minute. Stir in peas and turkey; heat through. Remove from heat; stir in dill, if you like.

4 Spoon turkey mixture into four deep dinner plates; top with biscuits. Or serve shortcake-style: split biscuits horizontally and spoon turkey between halves.

TIP Who says shortcakes are for dessert? For extra kick, we added black pepper to these shortcake biscuits. The dill is wonderfully fragrant in the sauce, but an equal amount of chopped fresh parsley, basil, or chives would also work well with the turkey and vegetables.

EACH SERVING: ABOUT 490 CALORIES | 31G PROTEIN | 51G CARBOHYDRATE | 17G TOTAL FAT (4G SATURATED) | 5G FIBER | 61MG CHOLESTEROL | 1,065MG SODIUM

③ TURKEY VEGETABLE SOUP

Delicious and soul-satisfying, our homemade Turkey Vegetable Soup is made hearty with rice, fresh corn, and frozen lima beans (see Tip).

ACTIVE TIME: 15 MINUTES · **TOTAL TIME:** 35 MINUTES
MAKES: 4 MAIN-DISH SERVINGS

---

1   TABLESPOON BUTTER OR MARGARINE

1   MEDIUM ONION, CHOPPED

3   MEDIUM CARROTS, CUT INTO ½-INCH CHUNKS

2   MEDIUM STALKS CELERY, CUT INTO ½-INCH SLICES

1   CUP FROZEN LIMA BEANS

6   CUPS TURKEY BROTH (OPPOSITE)

¾   TEASPOON SALT

¼   TEASPOON GROUND BLACK PEPPER

2   CUPS COOKED RICE

1½ CUPS FRESH CORN KERNELS

2   CUPS (½-INCH CHUNKS) SKINLESS LEFTOVER COOKED TURKEY

½   CUP FRESH PARSLEY LEAVES, CHOPPED (OPTIONAL)

1 In 4-quart saucepan, melt butter on medium heat. Add onion and cook 6 minutes or until tender, stirring often.

2 Stir in carrots, celery, beans, broth, salt, and pepper; heat to boiling on high. Reduce heat to low and simmer 5 minutes or until vegetables are tender.

3 Stir rice and corn into soup; heat to boiling. Stir in turkey and heat through. Remove saucepan from heat; stir in parsley, if using. Makes about 12 cups.

TIP Vary the vegetables with the season: add a chopped late-summer tomato in the fall, or use frozen corn in the winter. If you don't have parsley, use a few celery leaves.

EACH SERVING: ABOUT 435 CALORIES │ 32G PROTEIN │ 58G CARBOHYDRATE │ 9G TOTAL FAT (2G SATURATED) │ 7G FIBER │ 62MG CHOLESTEROL │ 970MG SODIUM

TURKEY BROTH

Homemade broth is a wonderful addition to any home cook's repertoire. It can enrich everything from soups and stews to sautéed dishes, including our Turkey Vegetable Soup.

ACTIVE TIME: 15 MINUTES · **TOTAL TIME:** 4 HOURS PLUS COOLING

MAKES: ABOUT 4½ QUARTS

TURKEY CARCASS, SCRAPS, AND NECK FROM ROAST TURKEY (PAGE 48)

2 MEDIUM CARROTS, CUT INTO 2-INCH CHUNKS

1 LARGE ONION, CUT INTO QUARTERS

1 LARGE STALK CELERY, CUT INTO 2-INCH CHUNKS

¼ TEASPOON DRIED THYME

PARSLEY STEMS FROM 1 BUNCH

1 In 10- to 12-quart stockpot (if you don't have 1 pot large enough, divide ingredients between 2 smaller ones), combine turkey carcass, cut up if necessary, scraps, and neck with carrots, onion, celery, thyme, and parsley. Add enough *cold water* to just cover ingredients; heat to boiling on high. Reduce heat to low and simmer, uncovered, 3 hours.

2 Slowly and carefully pour turkey broth through colander into very large bowl set in sink. Discard solids.

3 To cool broth quickly before refrigerating, set bowl with broth in sink filled with ice water and stir broth occasionally until cool, adding additional ice to sink if necessary, about 1½ hours.

4 Cover bowl and refrigerate turkey broth overnight. Spoon off and discard fat. Refrigerate broth up to 3 days, or freeze in 1-quart portions to use within 6 months.

EACH CUP: ABOUT 20 CALORIES | 2G PROTEIN | 1G CARBOHYDRATE | 1G TOTAL FAT (0G SATURATED) | 0G FIBER | 5MG CHOLESTEROL | 65MG SODIUM

STRATEGY 3:
PASTA FOR YOUR CROWD

Pasta's remarkable capacity to feed a large number of people for a modest price is its most heartwarming credential. It's nutritious, easy to prepare, and delicious. Serve a big bowl of saucy pasta or a piping hot pan of mac and cheese and everyone is content, including the cook.

Whether you create one of our light and luscious pastas tossed with seasonal vegetables, chicken, or shrimp or bake a rich, layered casserole until it's golden and bubbling, pasta allows you to prepare suppers that are as satisfying as they are economical. To keep dinnertime interesting, we've included a recipe for pesto made with broccoli (instead of the usual basil) and a handful of noodle dishes featuring Asian flavors. However, we use dried Italian-style pasta for them all. Made from flour and water, dried pasta is economical, lower in fat than fresh pasta, and a good match for a variety of sauces.

Tired of pairing pasta with your usual side salad of lettuce routine? See Side Salad in a Snap, page 43. If you want to incorporate fresh herbs or greens into your pasta dishes (and we recommend it), see our wallet-friendly tips for selecting and storing them (pages 59 and 63).

Whole Wheat Penne Genovese (page 58)

CHICKEN BOLOGNESE

This affordable family dinner recipe combines lean ground chicken, linguine, and classic Bolognese ingredients.

ACTIVE TIME: 40 MINUTES · TOTAL TIME: 1 HOUR

MAKES: 6 MAIN-DISH SERVINGS

---

12 OUNCES LINGUINE OR FETTUCCINE

4 TEASPOONS OLIVE OIL

1 POUND GROUND CHICKEN BREAST

½ TEASPOON SALT

2 MEDIUM CARROTS, CHOPPED

2 MEDIUM STALKS CELERY, CHOPPED

1 LARGE (10- TO 12-OUNCE) ONION, CHOPPED

1 CLOVE GARLIC, CRUSHED WITH PRESS

1 CAN (28-OUNCE) CRUSHED TOMATOES

¼ TEASPOON FRESHLY GROUND BLACK PEPPER

½ CUP REDUCED-FAT (2%) MILK

⅓ CUP FRESHLY GRATED PARMESAN CHEESE

¼ CUP LOOSELY PACKED FRESH PARSLEY LEAVES, CHOPPED (OPTIONAL)

1 Heat large covered saucepot of *salted water* to boiling over high heat. Add pasta and cook as label directs.

2 Meanwhile, in 12-inch nonstick skillet, heat 2 teaspoons oil on medium 1 minute. Add ground chicken to skillet; sprinkle with ¼ teaspoon salt. Cook chicken 8 to 9 minutes, or until it is no longer pink, stirring occasionally. Transfer chicken along with any juices in skillet to medium bowl.

3 To same skillet, add remaining 2 teaspoons oil with carrots, celery, onion, and garlic; cook 10 to 12 minutes or until vegetables are lightly browned and tender, stirring occasionally. Stir in tomatoes, remaining ¼ teaspoon salt, and pepper; heat to boiling. Reduce heat to medium-low and simmer, uncovered, 10 minutes, stirring occasionally. Stir in cooked chicken and milk; heat through.

4 Reserve ¼ *cup pasta cooking water*. Drain pasta and return to saucepot; stir in sauce from skillet, Parmesan, parsley, if using, and reserved cooking water, and toss to coat.

EACH SERVING: ABOUT 410 CALORIES | 29G PROTEIN | 59G CARBOHYDRATE | 6G TOTAL FAT (2G SATURATED) | 5G FIBER | 49MG CHOLESTEROL | 800MG SODIUM

WHOLE WHEAT PENNE GENOVESE

An onion-flecked white bean sauté adds heft to this fresh and healthy pesto pasta dish, making it light yet satisfying. (See page 54 for photo.)

TOTAL TIME: 30 MINUTES

MAKES: 6 MAIN-DISH SERVINGS

---

12 OUNCES WHOLE WHEAT PENNE OR ROTINI

1½ CUPS PACKED FRESH BASIL LEAVES

1 CLOVE GARLIC

3 TABLESPOONS WATER

3 TABLESPOONS OLIVE OIL

¼ TEASPOON SALT

¼ TEASPOON FRESHLY GROUND BLACK PEPPER

½ CUP FRESHLY GRATED PECORINO ROMANO CHEESE

1 SMALL ONION (4 TO 6 OUNCES), CHOPPED

1 CAN (15 TO 19 OUNCES) WHITE KIDNEY BEANS (CANNELLINI), RINSED AND DRAINED

1 PINT GRAPE TOMATOES (RED, YELLOW, AND ORANGE MIX IF AVAILABLE), EACH CUT INTO QUARTERS

1   Heat large covered saucepot of *salted water* to boiling over high heat. Add pasta and cook as label directs.

2   Meanwhile, make pesto: In food processor with knife blade attached, blend basil, garlic, water, 2 tablespoons oil, salt, and pepper until pureed, stopping processor occasionally and scraping bowl with rubber spatula. Add Romano; pulse to combine. Set aside.

3   In 12-inch skillet, heat remaining 1 tablespoon oil on medium until very hot; add onion and cook 5 to 7 minutes or until beginning to soften. Stir in white beans, and cook 5 minutes longer, stirring occasionally.

4   Reserve ¼ cup *pasta cooking water*. Drain pasta and return to saucepot; stir in white bean mixture, pesto, cut-up tomatoes, and reserved cooking water. Toss to coat.

EACH SERVING: ABOUT 375 CALORIES | 15G PROTEIN | 59G CARBOHYDRATE | 10G TOTAL FAT (2G SATURATED) | 9G FIBER | 5MG CHOLESTEROL | 435MG SODIUM

WALLET-FRIENDLY TIPS: FRESH HERBS

It's a waste to spend up to $3 on a bundle of herbs, use a handful, and then ditch the bunch when it wilts. Next time, select herbs with a fresh fragrance and unblemished leaves. Use what you need in your recipe, then choose a way to save the rest for later.

In the refrigerator, most herbs stay fresh for up to five days. Wrap sprigs in a damp paper towel; place in an airtight plastic bag. Or put parsley, cilantro, or basil in a tall glass with 1 inch water, stem ends down. Cover with a plastic bag, and secure with a rubber band. Change the water every couple of days. Wash herbs and blot dry just before using.

Freezing preserves flavor, but the herbs tend to go limp and darken. So, use frozen herbs in cooked dishes, not for pretty garnishes. Before freezing, wash and thoroughly dry the herbs. Use without thawing first, in the same quantities as fresh herbs for cooking. To freeze:

- **Mint and chives:** Wrap in foil, place in freezer-safe zip-tight bag, and snip as needed.
- **Parsley, sage, and thyme:** Chop and freeze in airtight containers.
- **Whole sage, rosemary, and basil leaves:** Layer in coarse (kosher) salt to preserve, and store in airtight containers for up to six months. Brush off salt before using.

Or, puree herbs in a blender or food processor with a little water and freeze in ice-cube tray. Once frozen, store in a zip-tight bag and drop into soups, sauces, or stews for instant flavor. (Don't try this with rosemary; the flavor would be too concentrated.)

Another option is to dry them. Dried thyme, rosemary, sage, sweet marjoram, bay, dill, oregano, and lavender have almost as much flavor as when they're first picked—or even more. (Parsley, chives, basil, cilantro, tarragon, and chervil aren't worth drying.) Rinse; pat thoroughly dry, or shake water off in a salad spinner. Gather sprigs, and tie at base with string. Hang bunches upside down in a dry, well-ventilated room.

Allow four to ten days; the faster herbs dry, the more color and fragrance they'll retain. They're ready when the leaves are crisp and brittle. Store in a cool dark place for up to a year.

BUTTERNUT SQUASH LASAGNA

With freeze-now, serve-later dishes like this one, you can provide your family with a comfy meal on even the busiest weeknight.

ACTIVE TIME: 50 MINUTES · **TOTAL TIME:** 2 HOURS
MAKES: 2 LASAGNAS, 12 MAIN-DISH SERVINGS

- 2 LARGE ONIONS, EACH CUT IN HALF, THEN CUT CROSSWISE INTO ¼-INCH SLICES
- 2 TABLESPOONS OLIVE OIL
- 1½ TEASPOONS SALT
- ¾ TEASPOONS COARSELY GROUND BLACK PEPPER
- 2 MEDIUM BUTTERNUT SQUASH, EACH CUT IN HALF AND SEEDED
- 7 CUPS LOW-FAT (1%) MILK
- ½ CUP CORNSTARCH
- ¼ CUP PACKED FRESH SAGE LEAVES, CHOPPED (OPTIONAL)
- ¼ TEASPOON GROUND NUTMEG
- 2 CUPS FRESHLY GRATED PARMESAN CHEESE
- 12 NO-BOIL LASAGNA NOODLES, FROM 8- TO 9-OUNCE PACKAGE
- 3 PACKAGES (10 OUNCES EACH) FROZEN CHOPPED SPINACH, THAWED AND SQUEEZED DRY

1   Preheat oven to 450°F. In large bowl, toss onions with oil, ¼ teaspoon salt, and ¼ teaspoon pepper. Place onions in one 15½" by 10½" jelly-roll pan. Line a second jelly-roll pan with foil; arrange squash, cut sides up. Sprinkle with ¼ teaspoon salt and ¼ teaspoon pepper. Cover pan with squash tightly with aluminum foil. (Do not cover onions.) Roast both pans of vegetables 45 minutes or until squash is tender and onions are browned, stirring onions halfway through cooking. Reset oven control to 375°F.

2   Meanwhile, in 5-quart saucepot (do not use a smaller pot; milk mixture may boil over), heat 6 cups milk on medium-high heat just to simmering, stirring occasionally. In small bowl, whisk cornstarch into remaining 1 cup milk. Add cornstarch mixture to simmering milk in pot; heat to a full rolling boil, stirring constantly. (Make sure to scrape bottom of saucepot to prevent scorching.) Boil 1 minute, stirring constantly. Remove white sauce from heat; stir in sage, if using, nutmeg, 1½ cups Parmesan, and remaining 1 teaspoon salt and ¼ teaspoon pepper.

3   When vegetables are done, scrape squash into food processor with knife blade attached; discard skins. Add onions to processor; puree until smooth. You should have 4 cups puree.

4   Into each of two 8" by 8" glass or ceramic baking dishes, spoon ½ cup white sauce to cover bottoms. Arrange 2 lasagna noodles over sauce in each casserole. Evenly spread 1 cup squash puree, then ¾ cup chopped spinach over noodles in each casserole. Top each with 1 cup sauce. Repeat layering one time, starting with noodles. Top each with 2 more noodles. Spread remaining sauce over noodles; sprinkle with remaining ½ cup Parmesan.

5   Cover one casserole with aluminum foil. Place casserole on cookie sheet (to catch any spills during baking) in oven and bake 30 minutes. Uncover and bake 15 minutes longer or until hot and bubbly. Let stand 10 minutes for easier serving. Meanwhile, prepare second casserole for freezing (see Freeze Now, Serve Later Casseroles, page 69).

EACH SERVING: ABOUT 335 CALORIES | 17G PROTEIN | 46G CARBOHYDRATE | 10G TOTAL FAT (4G SATURATED) | 5G FIBER | 17MG CHOLESTEROL | 170MG SODIUM

FUSILLI WITH SWISS CHARD, GARBANZO BEANS, AND BACON

Dark-green Swiss chard is loaded with vitamins K, A, and C, as well as minerals; toss it into an already good-for-you bean and whole-grain pasta dish, and you've got a nutritional powerhouse. The single slice of bacon lends rich flavor without adding much fat.

ACTIVE TIME: 20 MINUTES · TOTAL TIME: 30 MINUTES
MAKES: 4 MAIN-DISH SERVINGS

12 OUNCES WHOLE WHEAT FUSILLI OR ROTINI PASTA

1 BUNCH SWISS CHARD OR SPINACH (1 POUND), TOUGH ENDS TRIMMED

1 SLICE BACON, CUT INTO ½-INCH-WIDE STRIPS

1 GARLIC CLOVE, CRUSHED WITH GARLIC PRESS

¼ TEASPOON CRUSHED RED PEPPER

1 CAN (15 TO 19 OUNCES) GARBANZO BEANS, RINSED AND DRAINED

½ TEASPOON SALT

2 TABLESPOONS FRESH LEMON JUICE

1 Heat large covered saucepot of *salted water* to boiling over high heat. Add pasta and cook as label directs.

2 Meanwhile, cut ribs and stems from Swiss chard leaves. Cut ribs and stems into 1-inch pieces; cut leaves into 2-inch pieces. Rinse Swiss chard in large bowl of cold water; swish to remove any dirt. Transfer to colander. Do not spin dry.

3 In 12-inch nonstick skillet, cook bacon over medium-high heat until browned, tossing occasionally. With slotted spoon, transfer bacon to paper towels to drain. Reduce heat to medium. To bacon fat in skillet, add garlic and crushed red pepper; cook 30 seconds, stirring. Add chard, beans, and salt. Cover and cook until chard begins to wilt, about 2 minutes. Uncover and cook until stems are tender-crisp, about 5 minutes longer.

4 Drain pasta, reserving *¼ cup pasta cooking water*. Return pasta to saucepot. Stir in Swiss chard mixture and lemon juice until combined. If mixture seems dry, add reserved pasta cooking water.

EACH SERVING: ABOUT 500 CALORIES | 21G PROTEIN | 93G CARBOHYDRATE | 8G TOTAL FAT (2G SATURATED) | 14G FIBER | 6MG CHOLESTEROL | 755MG SODIUM

WALLET-FRIENDLY TIPS: FRESH GREENS

Leafy greens such as Swiss chard, spinach, parsley, basil, and arugula are an inexpensive source of good nutrition. If you select greens carefully, then store them properly, most will keep fresh and crisp in the fridge for up to four days. Salad greens are highly perishable, so buy at a market that keeps them under refrigeration.

When ready to clean, discard any bruised, discolored, or wilted leaves and rinse. To dry greens, place them on a clean towel and gently pat dry or use a salad spinner.

To store greens, wrap in a damp cloth towel or between layers of damp paper towels, and place in a plastic bag or airtight container in the crisper.

Tear delicate greens by hand to avoid bruising. Other greens are also best torn, but can be cut with a stainless steel knife (carbon steel can cause "rusty" discoloration and alter the flavor).

FARFALLE WITH GRILLED FALL VEGETABLES

This vitamin-packed pasta is the perfect use for a bumper crop of zucchini or summer squash, whether you bought it for bargain prices or grew your own.

ACTIVE TIME: 10 MINUTES · **TOTAL TIME:** 35 MINUTES
MAKES: 4 MAIN-DISH SERVINGS

- 2 MEDIUM RED PEPPERS, EACH CUT LENGTHWISE INTO QUARTERS, SEEDS AND STEMS DISCARDED
- 2 MEDIUM (8 OUNCES EACH) ZUCCHINI AND/OR SUMMER SQUASH, CUT INTO ½-INCH-THICK DIAGONAL SLICES
- 1 MEDIUM ONION, CUT INTO 1½-INCH-THICK SLICES

- 2 TABLESPOONS OLIVE OIL
- ¼ TEASPOON SALT
- ¼ TEASPOON COARSELY GROUND BLACK PEPPER
- 1 POUND FARFALLE PASTA
- 2 LARGE TOMATOES, CHOPPED
- ⅓ CUP FRESHLY GRATED PECORINO ROMANO CHEESE PLUS ADDITIONAL FOR SERVING

1 Heat large covered saucepot of *salted water* to boiling over high heat.

2 Meanwhile, preheat outdoor grill for covered, direct grilling on medium. Place peppers, zucchini, and onion in large bowl; add oil, salt, and pepper. Toss until vegetables are evenly coated.

3 Place vegetables on hot grill grate; cover and cook 10 to 12 minutes or until vegetables are tender and lightly charred, turning over once. While vegetables are grilling, add pasta to boiling water and cook as label directs. As vegetables are done grilling, transfer to cutting board and coarsely chop.

4 Reserve ¼ cup *pasta cooking water*. Drain pasta. Return pasta and cooking water to saucepot; stir in tomatoes, grilled vegetables, and ⅓ cup Romano. Serve with additional Romano.

EACH SERVING: ABOUT 575 CALORIES | 20G PROTEIN | 100G CARBOHYDRATE | 11G TOTAL FAT (2G SATURATED) | 7G FIBER | 7MG CHOLESTEROL | 385MG SODIUM

SPAGHETTI CARBONARA PIE

Nothing's better on a chilly evening than this hearty pie.

ACTIVE TIME: 20 MINUTES · TOTAL TIME: 55 MINUTES PLUS STANDING
MAKES: 6 MAIN-DISH SERVINGS

---

12 OUNCES SPAGHETTI

6 SLICES (4 OUNCES) BACON, CUT INTO ¼-INCH PIECES

1 CONTAINER (15 OUNCES) PART-SKIM RICOTTA CHEESE

½ CUP GRATED PECORINO ROMANO CHEESE

2 LARGE EGGS

1 LARGE EGG YOLK

½ TEASPOON COARSELY GROUND BLACK PEPPER

1 PINCH NUTMEG

2 CUPS MILK

½ TEASPOON SALT

1 Preheat oven to 375°F. Heat large covered saucepot of *salted water* to boiling over high heat. Add spaghetti and cook as label directs.

2 Meanwhile, in nonstick 10-inch skillet, cook bacon over medium heat until browned, tossing occasionally, about 12 minutes. With slotted spoon, transfer bacon to paper towels to drain; set aside.

3 In blender at low speed, blend ricotta, Romano, eggs, egg yolk, pepper, nutmeg, ½ cup milk, and salt until smooth.

4 Drain pasta and return to saucepot. Add ricotta mixture, bacon, and remaining 1½ cups milk, stirring to combine.

5 Transfer pasta mixture to 2½-quart baking dish (about 2 inches deep). Bake 35 to 40 minutes until golden around edges and almost set but still slightly liquid in center. Let pie stand 10 minutes before serving (liquid will be absorbed during standing). Cut into wedges to serve.

EACH SERVING: ABOUT 470 CALORIES | 25G PROTEIN | 50G CARBOHYDRATE | 18G TOTAL FAT (9G SATURATED) | 0G FIBER | 154MG CHOLESTEROL | 595MG SODIUM

SAUSAGE AND PEPPER BAKED ZITI

Our cheesy baked ziti is studded with zesty Italian sausage.

ACTIVE TIME: 40 MINUTES · **TOTAL TIME:** 1 HOUR 20 MINUTES

MAKES: 2 CASSEROLES, 8 MAIN-DISH SERVINGS

- 1 POUND SWEET AND/OR HOT ITALIAN SAUSAGE LINKS, CASINGS REMOVED
- 4 CLOVES GARLIC, CRUSHED WITH PRESS
- 2 LARGE GREEN, RED, AND/OR YELLOW PEPPERS, CUT INTO 1¼-INCH SLICES
- 1 JUMBO (1-POUND) ONION, CUT IN HALF, THEN CUT CROSSWISE INTO ¼-INCH SLICES
- 1 POUND SLICED WHITE MUSHROOMS

- 1 CAN (28-OUNCE) WHOLE TOMATOES IN PUREE
- 1 CAN (15-OUNCE) TOMATO PUREE
- ½ TEASPOON SALT
- 1 PACKAGE (16 OUNCES) ZITI OR PENNE PASTA
- 1 PACKAGE (8 OUNCES) PART-SKIM MOZZARELLA CHEESE, SHREDDED (2 CUPS)
- ½ CUP FRESHLY GRATED PECORINO ROMANO CHEESE

1   In deep 12-inch nonstick skillet, cook sausage on medium heat 10 minutes or until browned, stirring and breaking it up with side of spoon. With slotted spoon, transfer sausage to medium bowl.

2   In drippings in skillet, cook garlic, peppers, onion, and mushrooms, covered, 10 minutes. Uncover and cook 8 minutes longer or until vegetables are tender and most of liquid has evaporated. Stir in tomatoes, tomato puree, and salt; heat to boiling on medium-high, stirring and breaking up tomatoes with side of spoon. Reduce heat to medium-low; cover and cook sauce 10 minutes, stirring occasionally. Meanwhile, heat large covered saucepot of *salted water* to boiling on high. Add pasta and cook 2 minutes less than label directs.

3   Preheat oven to 400°F. Reserve *½ cup pasta cooking water*. Drain pasta. Return pasta and reserved cooking water to pot; stir in tomato sauce to coat pasta. Add mozzarella and reserved sausage; toss to combine. Divide mixture evenly between two shallow ungreased 2½-quart ceramic baking dishes. Sprinkle with Romano. Bake one casserole 20 to 25 minutes or until top browns and sauce is bubbling. Let stand 10 minutes. Prepare second casserole for freezing (see Freeze Now, Serve Later Casseroles, page 69).

EACH SERVING: ABOUT 575 CALORIES | 28G PROTEIN | 63G CARBOHYDRATE | 24G TOTAL FAT (10G SATURATED) | 6G FIBER | 62MG CHOLESTEROL | 1,410MG SODIUM

MULTIGRAIN MAC AND CHEESE WITH CREAMY TOMATO-BASIL SAUCE

Mac and cheese is comfort food for your family *and* your wallet. We top this version with panko, bread crumbs traditionally used in Japanese cooking that produce a crisp, crunchy coating. Coarse cracker crumbs, such as those from saltines, make a good—and economical—topping, too.

ACTIVE TIME: 35 MINUTES · **TOTAL TIME:** 55 MINUTES
MAKES: 6 MAIN-DISH SERVINGS

---

1 PACKAGE (16 OUNCES) MULTIGRAIN OR WHOLE-WHEAT ROTINI OR PENNE PASTA

1 CAN (14½ OUNCES) DICED TOMATOES, DRAINED

2 TABLESPOONS BUTTER OR MARGARINE

1 CUP PANKO (JAPANESE-STYLE BREAD CRUMBS) OR CRACKER CRUMBS

¾ CUP FRESHLY GRATED PECORINO ROMANO CHEESE

1 SMALL ONION, CHOPPED

1 GARLIC CLOVE, FINELY CHOPPED

3 TABLESPOONS CORNSTARCH

4 CUPS REDUCED-FAT MILK (2%)

½ TEASPOON SALT

¼ TEASPOON GROUND BLACK PEPPER

10 OUNCES REDUCED-FAT SHARP CHEDDAR CHEESE (2%), SHREDDED (2½ CUPS)

1 CUP LOOSELY PACKED FRESH BASIL LEAVES, CHOPPED

---

1   Heat large covered saucepot of *water* to boiling over high heat. Add pasta and cook 2 minutes less than label directs. Drain pasta; transfer to large bowl. Stir in tomatoes; set aside.

2   Preheat oven to 375°F.

3   In microwave-safe small bowl, heat 1 tablespoon butter in microwave on High 20 seconds or until melted. Stir in cracker crumbs and ¼ cup Romano until blended; set aside.

4   Meanwhile, in 4-quart saucepan, melt remaining 1 tablespoon butter over medium heat; add onion and cook until tender and lightly browned, 6 to 8 minutes, stirring occasionally. Add garlic and cook 1 minute, stirring.

5   In large liquid measuring cup, whisk cornstarch into milk until blended. Whisk milk mixture, salt, and pepper into onion mixture in saucepan; heat to boiling over medium-high heat, stirring frequently. Boil sauce 1 minute to thicken slightly. Remove saucepan from heat and stir in Cheddar, basil, and remaining ½ cup Romano until cheeses melt. Stir cheese mixture into pasta mixture.

FREEZE NOW, SERVE LATER CASSEROLES

Cool in casserole pan, uncovered, at least 30 minutes in refrigerator or until just warm. Wrap tightly with heavy-duty foil; label and freeze up to 3 months.

At least 24 hours but no more than 2 days before reheating, place your frozen casserole in the refrigerator to thaw slightly.

To reheat in a conventional oven, unwrap the casserole. Loosely cover it with foil and bake according to the recipe's reheating instructions until the center of the casserole reaches 160°F (check with an instant-read thermometer).

To reheat in a microwave, unwrap the casserole; cover the top with waxed paper, tucking it under the dish (make sure it's microwave-safe) to keep in place, or use plastic wrap and turn back a corner to vent. Heat in microwave according to the recipe's heating instructions, first on Low (30%) until ice crystals are gone and you can easily insert knife into center of casserole. Then cook on High until food is heated through and the internal termperature of your casserole is 160°F on an instant-read thermometer.

TIP Don't be tempted to remove the carousel in your microwave to accommodate large casseroles—a microwave designed to rotate food won't do its job properly without turning. If a casserole is too large to fit comfortably in your microwave, reheat in the oven.

6 Transfer pasta mixture to six 1½-cup au gratin dishes or one 13" by 9" glass baking dish; top with crumb mixture. Bake until center is hot and top is lightly browned, about 20 minutes.

EACH SERVING: ABOUT 645 CALORIES | 34G PROTEIN | 82G CARBOHYDRATE | 21G TOTAL FAT (11G SATURATED) | 7G FIBER | 56MG CHOLESTEROL | 1,055MG SODIUM

BAKED PASTA E FAGIOLI

Our main-course version of this classic Italian soup is as satisfying—and thrifty—as the original. Don't forget to serve a fresh, crusty loaf of bread to sop up the sauce.

ACTIVE TIME: 20 MINUTES · TOTAL TIME: 35 MINUTES
MAKES: 6 MAIN-DISH SERVINGS

---

8   OUNCES (ABOUT 2 CUPS) MINI PENNE OR ELBOW PASTA

1   CAN (28 OUNCES) WHOLE TOMATOES IN PUREE

1   TABLESPOON OLIVE OIL

1   MEDIUM ONION, CHOPPED

1   STALK CELERY, CHOPPED

2   CLOVES GARLIC, CRUSHED WITH PRESS

2   CANS (15 TO 19 OUNCES) NAVY OR OTHER SMALL WHITE BEANS, RINSED AND DRAINED

1   CUP REDUCED-SODIUM CHICKEN BROTH

1¼ TEASPOONS GROUND BLACK PEPPER

1   PACKAGE (10 OUNCES) FROZEN CHOPPED SPINACH, THAWED AND SQUEEZED DRY

½   CUP FRESHLY GRATED ROMANO CHEESE

1   Preheat oven to 400°F. Heat large covered saucepot of *water* to boiling over high heat. Add pasta and cook 2 minutes less than label directs. Drain pasta, reserving ¼ *cup cooking water*. Return pasta to saucepot.

2   Meanwhile, drain tomatoes, reserving puree. Coarsely chop tomatoes.

3   In 4-quart saucepan, heat oil over medium heat until hot. Add onion and celery, and cook 9 to 10 minutes or until tender, stirring occasionally. Add garlic; cook 1 minute.

4   Stir in tomatoes with their puree, beans, broth, and pepper; heat to boiling over high heat. Reduce heat to medium; stir in spinach.

5   Add bean mixture, reserved pasta cooking water, and ¼ cup Romano to pasta in saucepot and toss until well mixed. Transfer pasta mixture to 3-quart glass or ceramic baking dish. Sprinkle with remaining ¼ cup Romano. Bake 15 minutes or until center is hot and top is golden.

EACH SERVING: ABOUT 350 CALORIES │ 20G PROTEIN │ 65G CARBOHYDRATE │ 6G TOTAL FAT (2G SATURATED) │ 12G FIBER │ 7MG CHOLESTEROL │ 945MG SODIUM

STRATEGY 4:
VEGETARIAN FOR A NIGHT

For generations, the mealtime mantra of mothers across America has been "Eat your vegetables!" As usual, Mom was right. In study after study, it has been shown that eating a diet rich in fruits, vegetables, whole grains, and legumes results in numerous health benefits. From reducing the incidence of diabetes, strokes, and some cancers to lowering blood cholesterol and triglyceride levels, a low-fat vegetarian diet earns top marks. In fact, it's one of the most effective lifestyle measures to stop the progression of coronary artery disease.

But budget-conscious dinners is the topic at hand, and for that, vegetarian principles earn top marks, too. Adding more produce and grains and fewer animal products to your diet is not only good for your health, it's undeniably good for your pocketbook, too. You don't have to declare yourself a vegetarian—or convince your family to give up meat entirely—to enjoy the benefits of cooking and serving some vegetarian dinners each week. Here we present an array of family-friendly recipes that are so delicious, no one will be asking where the meat is. From our meatless burgers, wraps, and tacos to our pastas, stir-fries, and stews, eating vegetarian for the night is a winning strategy. For ideas on how to buy veggies at bargain prices, check out Wallet-Friendly Tips: High-Yield Harvests (page 85).

Sweet Potato and Peanut Stew (page 82)

SOUTHWESTERN BLACK-BEAN BURGERS

Add a side of potato salad for a meatless meal everyone will enjoy. For an even easier weeknight meal, make a double batch and freeze uncooked burgers. Defrost 10 minutes, then cook until heated through, about 12 minutes, turning once.

ACTIVE TIME: 15 MINUTES · TOTAL TIME: 20 MINUTES
MAKES: 4 BURGERS

- 1   CAN (15 TO 19 OUNCES) BLACK BEANS, RINSED AND DRAINED
- 2   TABLESPOONS LIGHT MAYONNAISE
- ¼   CUP PACKED FRESH CILANTRO LEAVES, CHOPPED
- 1   TABLESPOON PLAIN DRIED BREAD CRUMBS
- ½   TEASPOON GROUND CUMIN
- ½   TEASPOON HOT PEPPER SAUCE
- NONSTICK COOKING SPRAY
- 1   CUP LOOSELY PACKED SLICED LETTUCE
- 4   MINI (4-INCH) WHOLE-WHEAT PITAS, WARMED
- ½   CUP MILD SALSA

1   In large bowl, with potato masher or fork, mash beans with mayonnaise until almost smooth (some lumps of beans should remain). Stir in cilantro, bread crumbs, cumin, and pepper sauce until combined. With lightly floured hands, shape bean mixture into four 3-inch round patties. Spray both sides of each patty lightly with nonstick cooking spray.

2   Heat skillet over medium heat until hot. Add patties and cook until lightly browned, about 3 minutes. With spatula, turn patties over, and cook 3 minutes longer or until heated through.

3   Arrange lettuce on pitas; top with burgers then salsa.

EACH BURGER WITH PITA: ABOUT 210 CALORIES | 13G PROTEIN | 42G CARBOHYDRATE
3G TOTAL FAT (0G SATURATED) | 13G FIBER | 0MG CHOLESTEROL | 715MG SODIUM

PORTOBELLO "CHEESE STEAK" WRAPS

A hearty hand-held meal wrapped in a pita and served gyro style. So good we bet no one will ask "Where's the meat?"

TOTAL TIME: 35 MINUTES

MAKES: 4 SANDWICHES

- 2 MEDIUM PORTOBELLO MUSHROOMS (ABOUT 4 OUNCES EACH), STEMS REMOVED
- 2 TABLESPOONS OLIVE OIL
- 2 MEDIUM GREEN OR YELLOW PEPPERS, THINLY SLICED
- 1 JUMBO SWEET ONION (1 POUND) SUCH AS VIDALIA OR WALLA WALLA, THINLY SLICED
- ½ TEASPOON SALT
- ¼ TEASPOON COARSELY GROUND BLACK PEPPER
- 2 TABLESPOONS WATER
- 1 TABLESPOON BALSAMIC VINEGAR
- 4 (7-INCH) POCKETLESS PITAS
- 8 OUNCES PART-SKIM MOZZARELLA CHEESE, SHREDDED (2 CUPS)

1 Preheat oven to 400°F. Heat nonstick 12-inch skillet over medium-high heat until hot. Brush both sides of mushrooms using 1 tablespoon oil. Add mushrooms to skillet and cook until tender and lightly browned, about 5 minutes on each side. Transfer mushrooms to cutting board and cut into ¼-inch-thick slices; set aside.

2 In same skillet, heat remaining 1 tablespoon oil over medium heat until hot. Add peppers, onion, salt, pepper, and water; cook, stirring frequently, until the vegetables are tender and golden, about 15 minutes. Stir in vinegar; remove skillet from heat. Gently stir in sliced portobellos.

3 Meanwhile, place pitas on large cookie sheet; sprinkle with mozzarella cheese. Heat pitas in oven until cheese has melted, about 5 minutes.

4 Roll each pita into a cone; tightly wrap bottom half of each with kitchen parchment or foil to help hold its shape and prevent leakage. Fill pita cones with warm mushroom mixture.

EACH SANDWICH: ABOUT 460 CALORIES | 24G PROTEIN | 52G CARBOHYDRATE | 18G TOTAL FAT (7G SATURATED) | 4G FIBER | 41MG CHOLESTEROL | 1,060 MG SODIUM

FALAFEL SANDWICHES

Serve these small, flat bean patties in pita pockets with lettuce, tomatoes, cucumbers, and tangy plain low-fat yogurt.

TOTAL TIME: 25 MINUTES

MAKES: 4 SANDWICHES

4   GREEN ONIONS, CUT INTO 1-INCH PIECES

2   CLOVES GARLIC, EACH CUT IN HALF

½   CUP PACKED FRESH FLAT-LEAF PARSLEY

2   TEASPOONS DRIED MINT

1   CAN (15 TO 19 OUNCES) GARBANZO BEANS, RINSED AND DRAINED

½   CUP PLAIN DRIED BREAD CRUMBS

1   TEASPOON GROUND CORIANDER

1   TEASPOON GROUND CUMIN

1   TEASPOON BAKING POWDER

½   TEASPOON SALT

¼   TEASPOON GROUND RED PEPPER, (CAYENNE)

¼   TEASPOON GROUND ALLSPICE

OLIVE OIL NONSTICK COOKING SPRAY

4   (6- TO 7-INCH) PITAS

ACCOMPANIMENTS: SLICED ROMAINE LETTUCE, SLICED TOMATOES, SLICED CUCUMBER, SLICED RED ONION, PLAIN LOW-FAT YOGURT

1   In food processor with knife blade attached, finely chop green onions, garlic, parsley, and mint. Add garbanzo beans, bread crumbs, coriander, cumin, baking powder, salt, ground red pepper, and allspice; blend until a coarse puree forms.

2   Shape bean mixture, by scant ½ cups, into eight 3-inch round patties and place on sheet of waxed paper. Spray both sides of patties with olive oil spray.

3   Heat nonstick 10-inch skillet over medium-high heat until hot. Add half of patties and cook 8 minutes or until dark golden brown, turning once. Transfer patties to paper towels to drain. Repeat with remaining patties.

4   Cut off top third of each pita to form a pocket. Place warm patties in pitas. Serve with choice of accompaniments.

EACH SANDWICH WITHOUT ACCOMPANIMENTS: ABOUT 365 CALORIES | 14G PROTEIN 68G CARBOHYDRATE | 5G TOTAL FAT (1G SATURATED) | 9G FIBER | 0MG CHOLESTEROL 1,015MG SODIUM

QUESO BLANCO SOFT TACO

These tacos are filled with queso blanco, a white cheese that's a bit firmer than mozzarella, so it holds its shape when melted. Don't confuse it with queso fresco, a crumbly fresh cow's milk cheese that's found in almost every Latin American country.

ACTIVE TIME: 20 MINUTES · **TOTAL TIME:** 25 MINUTES
MAKES: 4 MAIN-DISH SERVINGS

- 3 GREEN ONIONS, THINLY SLICED
- 3 PLUM TOMATOES, CUT INTO ½-INCH PIECES
- 1 RIPE AVOCADO, PEELED, PITTED, AND CUT INTO ½-INCH PIECES
- ¼ SMALL HEAD ROMAINE LETTUCE, THINLY SLICED (2 CUPS)
- ¼ CUP LOOSELY PACKED FRESH CILANTRO LEAVES (OPTIONAL)
- 1 CUP MILD OR MEDIUM-HOT SALSA
- 1 PACKAGE (12 OUNCES) QUESO BLANCO (MEXICAN FRYING CHEESE), CUT INTO 12 SLICES
- 12 (6-INCH) CORN TORTILLAS, WARMED
- 1 LIME, CUT INTO 4 WEDGES

1 On platter, arrange green onions, tomatoes, avocado, lettuce, and cilantro, if using. Pour salsa into serving bowl.

2 Heat nonstick 12-inch skillet over medium-high heat until hot. Add cheese and heat 2 to 3 minutes or until dark brown in spots, turning over once.

3 Place 1 slice cheese in each tortilla and fold in half. Serve tortillas immediately, adding green onions, tomatoes, avocado, lettuce, cilantro, if using, salsa, and a squeeze of lime juice.

EACH SERVING: ABOUT 545 CALORIES | 26G PROTEIN | 49G CARBOHYDRATE | 29G TOTAL FAT (13G SATURATED) | 9G FIBER | 60MG CHOLESTEROL | 1,300MG SODIUM

STIR-FRIED TOFU WITH VEGETABLES

Choose extrafirm tofu for this dish: it won't fall apart when stir-fried. Serve over hot fluffy rice. (Because it takes 20 minutes to cook, start the rice as soon as you step into the kitchen.)

ACTIVE TIME: 20 MINUTES · **TOTAL TIME:** 30 MINUTES
MAKES: 4 MAIN-DISH SERVINGS

- 3 TABLESPOONS SOY SAUCE
- 1 TABLESPOON BROWN SUGAR
- 1 CUP WATER
- 2 TEASPOONS VEGETABLE OIL
- 3 GARLIC CLOVES, CRUSHED WITH GARLIC PRESS
- 1 TABLESPOON GRATED, PEELED FRESH GINGER
- ⅛ TO ¼ TEASPOON CRUSHED RED PEPPER

- 12 OUNCES BROCCOLI FLOWERETS (ABOUT 4 CUPS FROM 1 HEAD), CUT INTO UNIFORM PIECES
- 8 OUNCES MUSHROOMS, THINLY SLICED
- 1 MEDIUM RED PEPPER, CUT INTO 1-INCH PIECES
- 1 PACKAGE (15 OUNCES) EXTRAFIRM TOFU, PATTED DRY AND CUT INTO 1-INCH CUBES
- 3 GREEN ONIONS, TRIMMED AND THINLY SLICED

1 In small bowl, with wire whisk, mix soy sauce, brown sugar, cornstarch, and water until blended; set aside.

2 In deep nonstick 12-inch skillet, heat oil over medium-high heat until hot. Add garlic, ginger, and crushed red pepper; cook, stirring frequently (stir-frying), 30 seconds. Add broccoli, mushrooms, and red pepper; cook, covered, 8 minutes, stirring occasionally.

3 Add tofu and green onions and cook, uncovered, 2 minutes, stirring occasionally. Stir soy-sauce mixture to blend and add to skillet; heat to boiling. Boil, stirring, 1 minute.

EACH SERVING: ABOUT 225 CALORIES | 16G PROTEIN | 23G CARBOHYDRATE | 9G TOTAL FAT (1G SATURATED) | 5G FIBER | 0MG CHOLESTEROL | 775MG SODIUM

WALLET-FRIENDLY TIPS: SOY

Tofu is a bargain if you're looking for a low-fat, economical source of protein. At just 60 percent of the cost of chicken breasts, tofu is a versatile choice that can be used in a wide variety of your favorite stir-fries, noodle dishes, and casseroles, too.

Soy has been linked to health benefits ranging from a reduced risk of heart disease to stronger bones and fewer hot flashes. But an occasional veggie burger isn't enough. The FDA says you need to eat at least 25 grams of soy protein daily and follow a diet low in cholesterol and saturated fat to enjoy all the benefits. Consider adding other whole soy food such as soy milk, edamame (green soybeans), and soy nuts to your diet.

SWEET POTATO AND PEANUT STEW

A tasty and economical vegetarian dish with tomatoes, warm spices, and a touch of peanut butter. Microwaving the sweet potatoes helps you finish in a flash. (See page 72 for photo.)

ACTIVE TIME: 20 MINUTES · TOTAL TIME: 30 MINUTES
MAKES: 4 MAIN-DISH SERVINGS

- 3 LARGE SWEET POTATOES (12 OUNCES EACH), WELL SCRUBBED AND EACH CUT INTO 1½-INCH CHUNKS
- 1 TABLESPOON OLIVE OIL
- 2 GARLIC CLOVES, CRUSHED WITH GARLIC PRESS
- 1½ TEASPOONS GROUND CUMIN
- ½ TEASPOON SALT
- ¼ TEASPOON GROUND CINNAMON
- ⅛ TEASPOON CRUSHED RED PEPPER
- 2 CANS (15 TO 19 OUNCES EACH) GARBANZO BEANS, RINSED AND DRAINED
- 1 CAN (14 TO 14½ OUNCES) VEGETABLE BROTH (1¾ CUPS)
- 1 CAN (14½ OUNCES) DICED TOMATOES
- ¼ CUP CREAMY PEANUT BUTTER
- ½ CUP LOOSELY PACKED FRESH CILANTRO LEAVES, CHOPPED (OPTIONAL)

1   Place potatoes in 2½-quart microwave-safe dish. Cover dish and microwave on High about 8 minutes or until fork-tender.

2   Meanwhile, in 5- to 6-quart saucepot, heat oil over medium-high heat. Add garlic, cumin, salt, cinnamon, and crushed red pepper, and cook 30 seconds, stirring. Stir in beans, broth, tomatoes, and peanut butter until blended; heat to boiling and cook 1 minute, stirring occasionally.

3   Reduce heat to medium-low; add sweet potatoes to bean mixture and simmer 2 minutes, stirring occasionally. Stir in cilantro, if you like.

EACH SERVING: ABOUT 585 CALORIES | 22G PROTEIN | 92G CARBOHYDRATE | 16G TOTAL FAT (2G SATURATED) | 18G FIBER | 0MG CHOLESTEROL | 1,725MG SODIUM

LENTIL SHEPHERD'S PIE

A steaming skillet of Indian-spiced lentils are topped with piping-hot curried mashed sweet potatoes for this nonmeat takeoff on an old favorite.

ACTIVE TIME: 20 MINUTES · **TOTAL TIME:** 55 MINUTES
MAKES: 4 MAIN-DISH SERVINGS

- 1 CUP DRY LENTILS, RINSED
- 1 TABLESPOON GRATED, PEELED FRESH GINGER
- 1 TEASPOON GROUND CUMIN
- 1 CAN (14 TO 14½ OUNCES) VEGETABLE BROTH (1¾ CUPS)
- 1 BAY LEAF
- 1 TABLESPOON OLIVE OIL
- 1 TEASPOON CURRY POWDER
- ⅛ TEASPOON CRUSHED RED PEPPER
- 3 MEDIUM SWEET POTATOES (2 POUNDS), PEELED AND CUT INTO 1-INCH CHUNKS
- 1 TEASPOON SALT
- 2 GREEN ONIONS, THINLY SLICED
- PLAIN YOGURT (OPTIONAL)

1 In 12-inch skillet, place lentils, ginger, cumin, broth, bay leaf, and 1¼ *cups water*; heat to boiling over high heat. Reduce heat to medium; cover and cook 20 minutes or until lentils are tender. Discard bay leaf.

2 Meanwhile, in 3-quart saucepan, heat oil over medium-high heat until hot. Add curry powder and red pepper, and cook 15 seconds, stirring. Add sweet potatoes, salt, and ¾ *cup water*; heat to boiling. Reduce heat to medium-low; cover and cook 15 minutes or until potatoes are tender, stirring occasionally.

3 With potato masher or fork, mash potato mixture until almost smooth. Spoon mashed potatoes over lentil mixture in skillet; sprinkle with green onions. Serve with yogurt, if you like.

EACH SERVING: ABOUT 410 CALORIES | 18G PROTEIN | 77G CARBOHYDRATE | 5G TOTAL FAT (1G SATURATED) | 19G FIBER | 0MG CHOLESTEROL | 1,040MG SODIUM

COUSCOUS WITH GARBANZO BEANS

A vegetarian entrée fragrant with the flavors of Morocco—warm spices, green olives, and garlic—gets a quick start from seasoned couscous mix.

TOTAL TIME: 15 MINUTES

MAKES: 4 MAIN-DISH SERVINGS

- 1 BOX (5.6 OUNCES) COUSCOUS (MOROCCAN PASTA) WITH TOASTED PINE NUTS
- ⅓ CUP DARK SEEDLESS RAISINS
- 1 TABLESPOON OLIVE OIL
- 1 MEDIUM ZUCCHINI (10 OUNCES), CUT LENGTHWISE IN HALF, THEN CROSSWISE INTO ½-INCH-THICK SLICES
- 1 GARLIC CLOVE, CRUSHED WITH GARLIC PRESS
- ¾ TEASPOON GROUND CUMIN
- ¾ TEASPOON GROUND CORIANDER
- ⅛ TEASPOON GROUND RED PEPPER (CAYENNE)
- 2 CANS (15 TO 19 OUNCES EACH) GARBANZO BEANS, RINSED AND DRAINED
- ½ CUP SALAD OLIVES, DRAINED, OR CHOPPED PIMIENTO-STUFFED OLIVES
- ¼ CUP WATER

1 Prepare couscous as label directs except add raisins to *cooking water*.

2 Meanwhile, in nonstick 12-inch skillet, heat oil over medium-high until hot. Add zucchini and cook 5 minutes, stirring occasionally. Add garlic, cumin, coriander, and ground red pepper; cook 30 seconds, stirring. Add beans, olives, and water; cook 5 minutes, stirring often, until heated through.

3 Add cooked couscous to bean mixture and toss gently. Spoon into serving bowl.

EACH SERVING: ABOUT 555 CALORIES | 20G PROTEIN | 101G CARBOHYDRATE | 10G TOTAL FAT (1G SATURATED) | 15G FIBER | 0MG CHOLESTEROL | 1,110MG SODIUM

WALLET-FRIENDLY TIPS: HIGH-YIELD HARVESTS

Local fruits and veggies are always cheapest, so look for supermarket signs for seasonal produce from nearby farms, or shop farmers' markets and roadside stands. Bulk purchasing lowers costs even more (see our handy freeze-anything guide, page 152).

Hit the frozen-foods aisle for out-of-season produce that's affordable and full of flavor, as it's picked at its peak. Just bypass the pricey sweetened fruits or seasoned vegetables, and shop the store brand. Also a deal: canned veggies, especially tomatoes—a 28-ounce can delivers top taste for $1 less than the price of a pound of fresh.

Put in a little time slicing and dicing, and spend a lot less money on produce: whole veggies and fruits can run a dollar less per pound than the precut versions. See page 150 for a cheap-versus-convenient comparison.

CABBAGE AND BULGUR CASSEROLE

We layered Napa cabbage with a filling that is healthy and tastes good.

ACTIVE TIME: 45 MINUTES · **TOTAL TIME:** 1 HOUR 25 MINUTES
MAKES: 6 MAIN-DISH SERVINGS

2 CUPS WATER

1½ CUPS BULGUR

1 TABLESPOON VEGETABLE OIL

2 MEDIUM CARROTS, PEELED AND DICED

2 MEDIUM STALKS CELERY, DICED

1 MEDIUM RED PEPPER (4 TO 6 OUNCES), DICED

½ SMALL HEAD NAPA CABBAGE (CHINESE CABBAGE), CORED AND CUT CROSSWISE INTO 2-INCH STRIPS

3 GARLIC CLOVES, CRUSHED WITH GARLIC PRESS

3 GREEN ONIONS, SLICED

2 TABLESPOONS MINCED, PEELED FRESH GINGER

2 TABLESPOONS PLUS 1 TEASPOON SOY SAUCE

2 TABLESPOONS SEASONED RICE VINEGAR

1 CAN (14½ OUNCES) DICED TOMATOES

2 TABLESPOONS BROWN SUGAR

2 TABLESPOONS CHOPPED FRESH PARSLEY FOR GARNISH (OPTIONAL)

1 Preheat oven to 350°F.

2 In 2-quart saucepan, heat 1½ cups water to boiling over high heat; stir in bulgur. Remove saucepan from heat; cover and set aside.

3 In 5-quart Dutch oven, heat oil over medium-high heat. Add carrots, celery, and red pepper; cook 5 minutes. Add cabbage stems, and cook until vegetables are tender, 7 minutes longer. Reduce heat to low; add garlic, green onions, and ginger, and cook 1 minute longer, stirring.

4 Add remaining ½ cup water; heat to boiling over high heat. Reduce heat to low; simmer 1 minute, stirring. Remove Dutch oven from heat; stir in 2 tablespoons soy sauce, 1 tablespoon vinegar, and cooked bulgur.

5 In small bowl, combine tomatoes with their juice, brown sugar, and remaining 1 teaspoon soy sauce and 1 tablespoon vinegar.

6 In 3-quart casserole, place half of cabbage leaves; top with bulgur mixture, then remaining cabbage leaves. Spoon tomato mixture over top. Cover casserole and bake until hot in center and top layer of cabbage leaves is wilted, about 40 minutes. Sprinkle with parsley before serving.

EACH SERVING: ABOUT 220 CALORIES | 7G PROTEIN | 43G CARBOHYDRATE | 3G TOTAL FAT (0G SATURATED) | 12G FIBER | 0MG CHOLESTEROL | 800MG SODIUM

WALLET-FRIENDLY TIPS: WHOLE GRAINS

There's no better budget stretcher than cooking with whole grains. At a dollar or two per pound, pearl barley, brown rice, and bulgur are low in fat, high in protein, and tummy-filling. And there are lots of other interesting whole grains to sample—from wheat berries to millet to farro. Combine any of these with meat or veggies to make a little go a long, healthy way.

A box of rice pilaf will set you back a couple dollars and yield three cups, or one meal. Spend a dollar more on a five-pound bag of rice, and get the equivalent of 50 cooked cups. Mix with onions and chicken broth for DIY pilaf.

STRATEGY 5:
BREAKFAST FOR DINNER

Who doesn't love eating breakfast for dinner? An omelet with a zesty filling or a stack of pancakes for supper feels indulgent (even a bit naughty). But we're here to tell you that tucking into breakfast for dinner can be a money-wise and health-conscious strategy. After all, when you think of breakfast, the first thing that comes to mind is eggs, one of nature's most nutrient-rich and versatile foods. Not only are eggs an inexpensive protein source, they provide a tasty base for using up leftover meat, veggies, cheese, and herbs. And for added convenience, most egg recipes can be easily doubled. What's not to like about that?

In the pages that follow, you'll find recipes for eggs baked in frittatas and soufflés; scrambled in an assortment of omelets (step-by-step photos included); and poached and served on top of English muffins, black beans, or polenta with sauce. And then there are the pancakes, including sweet and thoroughly grown-up savory options, crêpes, and even a strata, a savory, custardy Italian-style baked bread pudding that turns stale bread into a thing of beauty. Tips on selecting and storing eggs and dairy increase your thriftiness quotient and the quality of your finished dishes, too.

The Perfect Cheese Omelet (page 90)

THE PERFECT CHEESE OMELET

Simple, versatile, and nutritious, omelets are the perfect fallback supper. Because the cooking time is so short, you'll need to have your eggs, seasonings, and fillings at your elbow so you can give individual attention to each omelet. (See page 88 for photo.)

ACTIVE TIME: 2½ MINUTES PER OMELET · TOTAL TIME: 18 MINUTES
MAKES: 4 OMELETS

8   LARGE EGGS (SEE TIP)

½   TEASPOON SALT

½   TEASPOON GROUND PEPPER

2   TABLESPOONS BUTTER OR MARGARINE

4   OUNCES CHEDDAR, GRUYÈRE, OR FONTINA CHEESE, SHREDDED (1 CUP) OR TOPPING OF CHOICE (SEE THREE OMELET SUPPERS, PAGE 92)

CHOPPED GREEN ONIONS FOR GARNISH

TOASTED COUNTRY-STYLE BREAD (OPTIONAL)

1   Preheat oven to 200°F. Place four dinner plates in oven to warm. In medium bowl, place eggs, water, salt, and pepper. With fork, beat 25 to 30 quick strokes to blend mixture without making it fluffy. (Overbeating toughens the proteins in the whites.)

2   In 8-inch nonstick skillet, melt 1½ teaspoons butter over medium heat. When butter stops sizzling, pour or ladle ½ cup egg mixture into skillet.

3   After egg mixture begins to set around edges, 25 to 30 seconds, with heat-safe spatula, carefully push cooked egg from side of skillet toward center, so uncooked egg can reach bottom of hot skillet. Repeat 8 to 10 times around skillet, tilting as necessary, 1 to 1½ minutes.

4   Cook until omelet is almost set but still creamy and moist on top. Position skillet so handle faces you, and sprinkle ¼ cup cheese (or topping of choice) on half of omelet.

5   With spatula, fold unfilled half over filling.

6   Shake pan gently to loosen any egg or filling from edge, then slide omelet to edge of skillet. Holding skillet above warm plate, tip skillet so omelet slides onto plate. Keep warm in oven. Repeat with remaining butter, egg mixture, and cheese or other filling to make 4 omelets in all. Sprinkle with green onions and serve with toast, if you like.

TIP For lighter omelets, substitute four large eggs and eight large egg whites.

EACH SERVING: ABOUT 315 CALORIES | 20G PROTEIN | 2G CARBOHYDRATE | 25G TOTAL FAT
(10G SATURATED) | 0G FIBER | 455MG CHOLESTEROL | 670MG SODIUM

THREE OMELET SUPPERS

It's simple: Prepare one of these tasty fillings. Then prepare The Perfect Cheese Omelet (page 90), but in step 4, instead of adding cheese, add your filling.

BLACK BEAN AND SALSA OMELETS

In nonstick 10-inch skillet, heat **1 cup canned black beans**, rinsed and drained, and **1 cup medium-hot salsa** over medium-high heat until all liquid evaporates, stirring often. Divide black-bean mixture, **1 medium avocado**, peeled and diced, and **¼ cup sour cream** among omelets.

ABOUT 350 CALORIES, 25G FAT PER OMELET

CREAMY MUSHROOM OMELETS

In nonstick 10-inch skillet, heat 1 tablespoon butter or margarine over medium-high heat. Add **1 medium onion**, minced; cook 5 minutes. Stir in **8 ounces mushrooms**, thinly sliced, **¼ teaspoon salt**, and **⅛ teaspoon pepper**; cook until liquid evaporate. Stir in **¼ cup heavy cream**; boil 3 minutes. Stir in 2 tablespoons **chopped parsley**.

ABOUT 285 CALORIES, 23G FAT PER OMELET

GARDEN VEGETABLE OMELETS

In nonstick 10-inch skillet, heat **1 tablespoon olive** oil over medium heat. Add **1 small onion**, chopped, **1 small zucchini** (6 ounces), chopped, **1 small yellow pepper**, chopped, **½ teaspoon salt**, and **⅛ teaspoon black pepper**; cook until tender. Add **2 plum tomatoes**, chopped, and **1¼ cup chopped fresh basil**; heat through.

ABOUT 245 CALORIES, 18G FAT PER OMELET

FLORENTINE FRITTATA

This frittata is a cheesy wonder, combining the smooth creaminess of mozzarella and the salty tang of feta.

TOTAL TIME: 20 MINUTES

MAKES: 4 MAIN-DISH SERVINGS

---

4 LARGE EGGS

4 LARGE EGG WHITES

1 PACKAGE (10 OUNCES) FROZEN CHOPPED SPINACH, THAWED AND SQUEEZED DRY

2 GREEN ONIONS, THINLY SLICED

¼ CUP CRUMBLED FETA CHEESE

3 OUNCES PART-SKIM MOZZARELLA CHEESE, SHREDDED (¾ CUP)

¼ TEASPOON SALT

1 TABLESPOON OLIVE OIL

1 CUP GRAPE OR CHERRY TOMATOES

1   Preheat broiler.

2   In large bowl, with wire whisk or fork, beat whole eggs, egg whites, spinach, green onions, feta, ½ cup mozzarella, and salt until blended.

3   In broiler-safe nonstick 10-inch skillet, heat oil over medium heat until hot. Pour egg mixture into skillet; arrange tomatoes on top, pushing some down. Cover skillet and cook frittata until egg mixture just sets around edge, 5 to 6 minutes.

4   Place skillet in broiler 5 to 6 inches from source of heat and broil frittata until just sets in center, 4 to 5 minutes. Sprinkle with remaining ¼ cup mozzarella; broil until cheese melts, about 1 minute longer.

5   To serve, gently slide frittata out of skillet and onto serving plate; cut into wedges.

EACH SERVING: ABOUT 230 CALORIES | 18G PROTEIN | 6G CARBOHYDRATE | 14G TOTAL FAT (6G SATURATED) | 2G FIBER | 233MG CHOLESTEROL | 570MG SODIUM

HEALTHY MAKEOVER EGGS BENEDICT

Velvety, egg-and-butter-rich hollandaise make Eggs Benedict irresistible, but unkind to both arteries and waistlines. We lightened it with a lemony white sauce and bumped up the fiber with spinach and whole-wheat muffins, so you can happily serve this brunch favorite for dinner.

ACTIVE TIME: 35 MINUTES · TOTAL TIME: 45 MINUTES

MAKES: 4 MAIN-DISH SERVINGS

1	LEMON	4	SLICES (4 OUNCES) LOW-SODIUM HAM
2	TABLESPOONS BUTTER OR MARGARINE	1	TABLESPOON DISTILLED WHITE VINEGAR
2	TABLESPOONS ALL-PURPOSE FLOUR	8	LARGE EGGS
1	CUP LOW-FAT (1%) MILK, WARMED	4	WHOLE-WHEAT ENGLISH MUFFINS
	PINCH SALT	1	SMALL BUNCH (10 OUNCES) SPINACH, TOUGH STEMS REMOVED
⅛	TEASPOON FRESHLY GROUND BLACK PEPPER	2	TEASPOONS SNIPPED CHIVES (OPTIONAL)

1 Preheat oven to 350°F. Fill teakettle with *water*; heat to boiling on high.

2 Meanwhile, prepare sauce: From lemon, grate ½ teaspoon peel and squeeze 2 tablespoons juice. In 1-quart saucepan, melt butter on low. Add flour and cook 1 minute, stirring. With wire whisk, gradually whisk in milk. Cook on medium, stirring, until sauce thickens and boils. Reduce heat; simmer, stirring, 5 minutes. Remove from heat; stir in lemon peel and juice, salt, and pepper. Keep warm. Makes 1 cup.

3 Meanwhile, halve ham slices; in 12-inch skillet, cook on medium 5 minutes, turning once. Remove; keep warm. To same skillet, add vinegar and *1½ inches boiling water*; keep at gentle simmer.

4 Break 1 egg into cup; holding cup at water's surface, slip in egg. Repeat with 3 more eggs; cook 3 to 5 minutes or until whites are set. With slotted spoon, transfer eggs to paper-towel-lined plate. Repeat with remaining eggs.

5 While eggs are cooking, toast muffin halves in oven until golden. Cook spinach as label directs. To serve, top each muffin half with 1 piece ham, one-eighth of spinach, 1 egg, and 2 tablespoons sauce. Sprinkle with chives, if using.

EACH SERVING: ABOUT 435 CALORIES | 32G PROTEIN | 35G CARBOHYDRATE | 19G TOTAL FAT (3G SATURATED) | 5G FIBER | 470MG CHOLESTEROL | 970MG SODIUM

WALLET-FRIENDLY TIPS: DAIRY

While the cost of eggs is rising, they're still a nutritional steal—eggs are one of the fastest ways to makeover leftovers or to quickly create filling dinners. Cartons of 18 are often marked down, since they're not as popular as the classic dozen.

It seems counterintuitive, but spending more for a pound of ultra-flavorful cheese like Gruyère or feta can actually save you cash. Because the taste is strong, you'll use less for cooking.

With a gallon of milk inching upward in price, why not try the powdered stuff for baking and cooking? A four-pound box of dry, nonfat milk costs twice as much but yields five gallons when reconstituted.

SPANISH TORTILLA WITH CHORIZO AND PEPPERS

A traditional Spanish dish, tortilla is a thick omelet composed of potato, onions, and egg. Our version also features spicy chorizo sausage and sautéed peppers.

ACTIVE TIME: 25 MINUTES · **TOTAL TIME:** 50 MINUTES
MAKES: 6 MAIN-DISH SERVINGS

1 POUND SMALL RED POTATOES, THINLY SLICED	8 LARGE EGGS
1 TEASPOON SALT	1 PACKAGE (3½-OUNCE) FULLY COOKED CHORIZO SAUSAGE, CUT INTO ¼-INCH PIECES
2 TABLESPOONS OLIVE OIL	
1 MEDIUM ONION, THINLY SLICED	¼ CUP (LOOSELY PACKED) FRESH PARSLEY LEAVES, CHOPPED (OPTIONAL)
1 RED OR GREEN PEPPER, THINLY SLICED	
1 CLOVE GARLIC, CRUSHED WITH PRESS	

1 In 2-quart saucepan, place potatoes with enough *water* to cover and 1 teaspoon salt; heat to boiling on high. Reduce heat to low and simmer 3 to 5 minutes or until tender when pierced with tip of knife. Drain potatoes; return to saucepan.

2 Meanwhile, preheat oven to 350°F. In 10-inch nonstick skillet with oven-safe handle, heat 1 tablespoon olive oil on medium 1 minute. Add onion, pepper, and garlic, and cook 12 minutes or until vegetables are tender and golden, stirring occasionally.

3 In large bowl, with fork, mix eggs, chorizo, and chopped parsley, if using, until well blended. Gently stir in potatoes and onion mixture.

4 In same skillet, heat remaining 1 tablespoon oil on medium. Pour in egg mixture and place in oven (see Tip). Bake 22 to 24 minutes or until knife inserted in center comes out clean and top is browned. Remove from oven.

5 Center large round plate upside down on top of skillet. Wearing oven mitts to protect your hands, and grasping plate and skillet firmly together, quickly invert tortilla onto plate. Slide onto cutting board to serve.

TIP If you don't have a nonstick skillet with an oven-safe handle, you can insulate your skillet's handle with a double thickness of foil before baking.

EACH SERVING: ABOUT 295 CALORIES | 18G PROTEIN | 20G CARBOHYDRATE | 18G TOTAL FAT (5G SATURATED) | 2G FIBER | 298MG CHOLESTEROL | 390MG SODIUM

HUEVOS RANCHEROS

This Mexican fried-egg dish is served with salsa, corn tortillas, and, if you choose, some avocado slices. It's a people-pleasing dish that's quick to make and easy on your budget.

ACTIVE TIME: 20 MINUTES · TOTAL TIME: 25 MINUTES

MAKES: 4 MAIN-DISH SERVINGS

---

1   TABLESPOON VEGETABLE OIL

1   MEDIUM ONION, FINELY CHOPPED

2   CLOVES GARLIC, CRUSHED WITH PRESS

1   TABLESPOON CHIPOTLE SAUCE OR OTHER HOT SAUCE PLUS ADDITIONAL FOR SERVING

1   TEASPOON GROUND CUMIN

1   CAN (28 OUNCES) TOMATOES IN JUICE, DRAINED AND CHOPPED

1   CAN (15 TO 19 OUNCES) BLACK BEANS, RINSED AND DRAINED

¼   CUP LOOSELY PACKED FRESH CILANTRO LEAVES, CHOPPED (OPTIONAL)

SALT

1   TABLESPOON BUTTER OR MARGARINE

4   LARGE EGGS

4   (6-INCH) CORN TORTILLAS, WARMED

1   AVOCADO, SLICED (OPTIONAL)

1   In 4-quart saucepan, heat oil on medium until hot. Add onion and garlic, and cook 8 minutes or until beginning to brown. Stir in chipotle sauce and cumin; cook 30 seconds, stirring. Add tomatoes; cover and cook 3 minutes to blend flavors, stirring occasionally. Stir in beans, half of cilantro, if using, and ¼ teaspoon salt; heat through, about 3 minutes, stirring occasionally.

2   Meanwhile, in 12-inch nonstick skillet, melt butter on medium. Crack eggs, 1 at a time, and drop into skillet. Cover skillet and cook eggs 4 to 5 minutes or until whites are set and yolks thicken.

3   Place tortillas on four dinner plates; top each with some tomato mixture and 1 egg. Sprinkle with remaining cilantro, if using. Serve with avocado and additional hot sauce, if you like.

EACH SERVING: ABOUT 315 CALORIES │ 15G PROTEIN │ 42G CARBOHYDRATE │ 12G TOTAL FAT (3G SATURATED) │ 10G FIBER │ 213MG CHOLESTEROL │ 765MG SODIUM

WALLET-FRIENDLY TIPS: EGGS

Always check the "use by" or "sell by" date on the egg carton; it is the clearest indication of freshness. The later the date, the longer you can use the eggs, and the fresher they are when you buy them. If there's no "use by" date (or to be extra sure the eggs are fresh), look for a "pack date," which appears on all USDA-inspected cartons. This three-digit number, ranging from 001 to 365 (corresponding to the days of the year), indicates the day on which the eggs were packed; they are safe to use for at least four to five weeks beyond this date.

The best way to store eggs for optimum quality is in their original carton on a low shelf in your refrigerator—not on the refrigerator door, even if it has a special egg-holder section. Older refrigerators with egg holders on the door invite constant temperature fluctuations each time the door is opened and closed, shortening the shelf life of eggs.

BAKED EGGS AND POLENTA WITH CHUNKY VEGETABLE SAUCE

Polenta makes a tasty—and unexpected—base for this saucy baked-egg casserole. (See page 6 for photo.)

ACTIVE TIME: 30 MINUTES · **TOTAL TIME:** 42 MINUTES
MAKES: 4 MAIN-DISH SERVINGS

1 CUP BOILING WATER	1 SMALL ONION, CHOPPED
1 CUP LOW-FAT MILK (1%)	1 SMALL ZUCCHINI (6 OUNCES), CHOPPED
½ CUP YELLOW CORNMEAL	1 CAN (14½ OUNCES) TOMATOES, CHOPPED
½ TEASPOON SALT	
½ CUP FRESHLY GRATED PECORINO ROMANO OR PARMESAN CHEESE	1 CAN (8 OUNCES) TOMATO SAUCE
1 TABLESPOON OLIVE OIL	¼ TEASPOON COARSELY GROUND BLACK PEPPER
1 MEDIUM CARROT, PEELED AND CHOPPED	4 LARGE EGGS

1 Prepare polenta: In deep 2½-quart microwave-safe bowl or casserole, stir boiling water, milk, cornmeal, and salt. Cook, uncovered, in microwave on High 3 minutes. Remove bowl from microwave and whisk cornmeal mixture vigorously until smooth (mixture may be lumpy at first). Microwave 2 to 3 minutes longer or until thickened, whisking once more after cooking is done. Stir in Romano. Spread polenta in greased 8-inch square glass baking dish.

2 Meanwhile, preheat oven to 400°F.

3 Prepare sauce: In 12-inch skillet, heat oil over medium heat until hot. Add carrot and onion, and cook until tender and beginning to brown, about 10 minutes. Stir in zucchini and cook just until zucchini is tender, about 5 minutes. Add tomatoes with their juice, tomato sauce, and pepper; heat to boiling over medium-high heat. Reduce heat to medium and cook 5 minutes, stirring occasionally. Spread tomato mixture over polenta in baking dish.

4 With large spoon, make 4 indentations in tomato mixture. Crack eggs into custard cup, one at a time, and slip into each indentation. Bake until eggs are set, 12 to 14 minutes.

EACH SERVING: ABOUT 290 CALORIES | 16G PROTEIN | 29G CARBOHYDRATE | 13G TOTAL FAT (4G SATURATED) | 4G FIBER | 223MG CHOLESTEROL | 1,325MG SODIUM

SPINACH SOUFFLÉ

Even though this recipe requires about 40 minutes total, only 20 minutes is active prep. During the remaining 20 minutes, while the soufflé bakes, you can relax!

ACTIVE TIME: 20 MINUTES · TOTAL TIME: 40 MINUTES

MAKES: 4 MAIN-DISH SERVINGS

---

3 TABLESPOONS PLAIN DRIED BREAD CRUMBS

COOKING SPRAY

1½ CUPS 1% LOW-FAT MILK

⅓ CUP CORNSTARCH

2 LARGE EGGS, SEPARATED

1 PACKAGE (10 OUNCES) FROZEN CHOPPED SPINACH, THAWED AND SQUEEZED DRY

3 TABLESPOONS GRATED PECORINO ROMANO OR PARMESAN CHEESE

½ TEASPOON SALT

¼ TEASPOON COARSELY GROUND BLACK PEPPER

½ TEASPOON CREAM OF TARTAR

4 LARGE EGG WHITES, OR POWDERED EGG WHITES (SEE TIP)

---

1   Preheat oven to 425°F. Spray 10-inch quiche dish or shallow 2-quart casserole with cooking spray; sprinkle with bread crumbs to coat. Set aside.

2   In 2-quart saucepan, with wire whisk, beat milk with cornstarch until blended. Heat milk mixture over medium-high heat until mixture thickens and boils, stirring constantly. Boil 1 minute. Remove saucepan from heat.

3   In large bowl, with rubber spatula, mix egg yolks, spinach, Romano, salt, and pepper until blended; stir in warm milk mixture. Cool slightly (if spinach mixture is too warm, it will deflate beaten egg whites).

4   In another large bowl, with mixer at high speed, beat cream of tartar and 6 egg whites until stiff peaks form. Gently fold egg-white mixture, one-third at a time, into spinach mixture.

5   Spoon soufflé mixture into quiche dish. Bake soufflé 20 minutes or until top is golden and puffed. Serve immediately.

TIP If using powdered egg whites, reconstitute following package directions. Powdered egg whites are available in the baking section of most supermarkets.

EACH SERVING: ABOUT 195 CALORIES | 15G PROTEIN | 23G CARBOHYDRATE | 5G TOTAL FAT (2G SATURATED) | 0G FIBER | 114MG CHOLESTEROL | 590MG SODIUM

BROCCOLI AND CHEDDAR CRÊPES

Serve these cheesy broccoli-stuffed crêpes with a mixed green salad for a satisfying dinner.

ACTIVE TIME: 45 MINUTES · TOTAL TIME: 1 HOUR
MAKES: 6 MAIN-DISH SERVINGS

---

3 LARGE EGGS	1 SMALL RED ONION, SLICED
⅔ CUP ALL-PURPOSE FLOUR	2 TABLESPOONS CORNSTARCH
3 CUPS REDUCED-FAT (2%) MILK	2 PACKAGES (10 OUNCES EACH) FROZEN CHOPPED BROCCOLI, THAWED
4 TABLESPOONS BUTTER OR MARGARINE, MELTED	1 PACKAGE (8 OUNCES) SHARP CHEDDAR CHEESE, SHREDDED (2 CUPS)
¾ TEASPOON SALT	¼ CUP LOOSELY PACKED FRESH PARSLEY LEAVES, CHOPPED (OPTIONAL)
¼ TEASPOON COARSELY GROUND BLACK PEPPER	

1 In blender, combine eggs, flour, 1½ cups milk, 2 tablespoons butter, and ½ teaspoon salt. Cover and blend until smooth, scraping down sides of blender occasionally. Transfer batter to medium bowl; cover and refrigerate at least 1 hour or overnight to allow flour to absorb liquid.

2 Lightly brush 10-inch nonstick skillet with some melted butter and heat on medium 1 minute. With wire whisk, thoroughly mix batter to blend well. Pour scant ¼ cup batter into skillet; tilt pan to coat bottom completely with batter. Cook crêpe until top is dry and set and underside is lightly browned, about 2 minutes.

3 With spatula, loosen edge of crêpe; turn crêpe over. Cook 30 seconds to 1 minute or until second side is browned. Slip crêpe onto waxed paper. Repeat with remaining batter, brushing pan lightly with butter before cooking each crêpe and stacking crêpes between layers of waxed paper. You should have at least 12 crêpes.

4 Meanwhile, preheat oven to 400°F. In 12-inch nonstick skillet, heat remaining tablespoon butter on medium until hot. Add onion and cook 6 to 8 minutes or until tender and beginning to brown. In cup, stir together cornstarch and remaining 1½ cups milk. To onion in skillet, add milk mixture, broccoli, remaining ¼ teaspoon salt, and pepper. Heat to boiling; boil 1 minute. Remove skillet from heat; stir in 1½ cups Cheddar.

5 Place crêpes on work surface; spread generous ¼ cup broccoli mixture on half of each crêpe. Starting from side with broccoli, roll up crêpes and place, seam side down, in shallow 2-quart glass or ceramic baking dish. Sprinkle with remaining ½ cup Cheddar.

6 Bake about 15 minutes or until cheese melts and crêpes are heated through. Sprinkle with parsley, if you like.

TIP You can make the crêpes a day or two ahead; wrap well and refrigerate until you're ready to fill them.

EACH SERVING: ABOUT 415 CALORIES | 21G PROTEIN, | 26G CARBOHYDRATE | 25G TOTAL FAT (12G SATURATED) | 4G FIBER | 155MG CHOLESTEROL | 725MG SODIUM

SAVORY RICOTTA PANCAKES WITH TOMATO-CHARD SAUCE

Pancakes transcend breakfast when they're made with savory ricotta cheese and topped with a zesty tomato and Swiss chard sauce.

ACTIVE TIME: 1 HOUR · TOTAL TIME: 1 HOUR 10 MINUTES
MAKES: 4 MAIN-DISH SERVINGS

- 1   BUNCH (8 OUNCES) SWISS CHARD, TOUGH ENDS TRIMMED
- 1   TABLESPOON OLIVE OIL
- 1   MEDIUM ONION, CHOPPED
- 1   CLOVE GARLIC, CRUSHED WITH PRESS
- 1   TABLESPOON TOMATO PASTE
- 1   CAN (28 OUNCES) WHOLE TOMATOES IN PUREE, CHOPPED
- ½   TEASPOON SALT

- 3   LARGE EGGS, SEPARATED
- 1   CUP PART-SKIM RICOTTA CHEESE
- ⅓   CUP REDUCED-FAT (2%) MILK
- ½   CUP ALL-PURPOSE FLOUR
- ¼   TEASPOON BAKING POWDER
- 1   TABLESPOON BUTTER OR MARGARINE, CUT INTO THREE PIECES
- ¼   CUP FRESHLY SHREDDED PECORINO ROMANO CHEESE

1   Cut ribs and stems from Swiss chard leaves. Cut ribs and stems into 1-inch pieces; cut leaves into 2-inch pieces. Rinse Swiss chard thoroughly in large bowl of cold water; swish to remove any dirt. With hands, transfer chard to colander, leaving dirt in bottom of bowl. Repeat process, changing water until all dirt is removed.

2   Prepare Tomato-Chard Sauce: In 4-quart saucepan, heat oil on medium until hot. Add onion and garlic, and cook 6 to 8 minutes or until tender. Add tomato paste; cook 1 minute, stirring. Add tomatoes with their puree and ¼ teaspoon salt; heat to boiling on medium-high. Stir in Swiss chard; reduce heat to medium-low and simmer, covered, 10 minutes. Remove cover and cook 8 to 10 minutes longer or until chard is tender and sauce is thickened slightly, stirring occasionally. Remove saucepan from heat; cover to keep sauce warm.

3   Meanwhile, preheat oven to 200°F. Prepare Savory Ricotta Pancakes: In blender or food processor with knife blade attached, blend egg yolks, ricotta, and milk until smooth. Add flour, baking powder, and remaining ¼ teaspoon salt, and blend until smooth; transfer batter to 8-cup glass measure or medium bowl.

4   In small bowl, with mixer on high speed, beat egg whites just until stiff peaks form when beaters are lifted. With rubber spatula, fold beaten whites into batter.

5   In 12-inch nonstick skillet, melt 1 piece butter on medium heat. Drop batter by ¼ cups into skillet, making 4 to 5 pancakes at a time. Cook 3 to 4 minutes or until edges look dry and bottoms are browned. Turn pancakes over, and cook 2 to 3 minutes or until bottoms are browned. Transfer pancakes to platter; keep warm in oven.

6   Repeat with remaining butter and batter to make about 16 pancakes in all. Serve pancakes with warm Tomato-Chard Sauce; sprinkle with shredded Romano.

EACH SERVING: ABOUT 350 CALORIES | 19G PROTEIN | 31G CARBOHYDRATE | 17G TOTAL FAT (6G SATURATED) | 3G FIBER | 185MG CHOLESTEROL | 1,155MG SODIUM

STRATEGY 6:
A BIG HEARTY POT OF SOUP

A steaming pot of soup or stew, slowly simmering on the stove, has come to symbolize the comforts of home. And for busy cooks with families on the go, soups and stews are a godsend: they require minimal prep work, they are made in one pot, and they have an astounding ability to stretch to feed more mouths than you counted on—just add some additional veggies or beans to the pot.

So what will it be tonight? Choose from our comforting favorites— think minestrone, beef stew, and chowder—or our more exotic offerings redolent with Caribbean, Cajun, or Asian seasonings. Whatever you choose, pair it with a crisp salad, add some crusty bread alongside, and your pot of soup will be transformed into a wholesome and complete meal. When possible, incorporate budget-conscious building blocks like our recipe for homemade chicken broth (page 108).

An added bonus for the cook: many soups taste even better the next day, which means leftovers are sure to be satisfying. Refrigerate or freeze them in individual-serving size containers to reheat for a quick meal. Even small amounts can serve as an accompaniment to a sandwich or salad. For additional tips, see Freeze Now, Serve Later Soups and Stews (page 109).

Winter Vegetable Chowder (page 118)

CHICKEN BROTH

Nothing beats the flavor of homemade chicken broth. Make it in large batches and freeze in sturdy containers for up to four months. Our recipe has an added bonus: the cooked chicken can be used in casseroles and salads. So rich, this broth can be used as a base for many of our soups and stews.

ACTIVE TIME: 20 MINUTES · **TOTAL TIME:** 4 HOURS 40 MINUTES PLUS COOLING
MAKES: ABOUT 5½ CUPS

- 1 CHICKEN (3 TO 3½ POUNDS), INCLUDING NECK (RESERVE GIBLETS FOR ANOTHER USE)
- 2 CARROTS, PEELED AND CUT INTO 2-INCH PIECES
- 1 STALK CELERY, CUT INTO 2-INCH PIECES
- 1 MEDIUM ONION, UNPEELED AND CUT INTO QUARTERS
- 5 PARSLEY SPRIGS
- 1 GARLIC CLOVE, UNPEELED
- ½ TEASPOON DRIED THYME
- ½ BAY LEAF

1 In 6-quart saucepot, combine chicken, chicken neck, carrots, celery, onion, parsley, garlic, thyme, bay leaf, and *3 quarts water* or enough *water* to cover; heat to boiling over high heat. With slotted spoon, skim foam from surface. Reduce heat to low; cover and simmer, turning chicken once and skimming foam occasionally, 1 hour.

2 Remove from heat; transfer chicken to large bowl. When cool enough to handle, remove skin and bones from chicken. (Reserve chicken meat for another use.) Return skin and bones to Dutch oven and heat to boiling over high heat. Skim foam; reduce heat to low and simmer, uncovered, 3 hours.

3 Strain broth through colander into large bowl; discard solids. Strain again through sieve into containers; cool. Cover and refrigerate to use within 3 days, or freeze up to 4 months.

4 To use, skim and discard fat from surface of broth.

EACH CUP: ABOUT 36 CALORIES | 3G PROTEIN | 4G CARBOHYDRATE | 1G TOTAL FAT (1G SATURATED) | 0G FIBER | 3MG CHOLESTEROL | 91MG SODIUM

PRESSURE-COOKER CHICKEN BROTH

In 6-quart pressure cooker, place all ingredients for Chicken Broth but use only 4 *cups water*. Following manufacturer's directions, cover pressure cooker and bring up to high pressure (15 pounds). Cook 15 minutes. Remove cooker from heat and allow pressure to drop 5 minutes, then follow manufacturer's directions for quick release of pressure. Strain broth through colander into large bowl; discard solids. Strain again through sieve into containers; cool. Meanwhile, remove skin and bones from chicken; discard. (Reserve chicken for another use.) Cover broth and refrigerate to use within 3 days, or freeze up to 4 months. To use, skim and discard fat from surface of broth.

FREEZE NOW, SERVE LATER SOUPS AND STEWS

Cool in containers, uncovered, at least 30 minutes in refrigerator or until warm. Cover containers tightly; label and freeze up to 4 months.

When ready to serve, place frozen soup or stew, still in covered containers, up to rim in bowl or sink of hot water 1 to 3 minutes or until sides separate from containers. Invert into saucepan or skillet; add ¼ to ½ cup water. Cover and heat to boiling over medium heat, stirring occasionally; boil 1 minute, stirring.

Or, invert into microwave-safe bowl or baking dish; cover with waxed paper or vented plastic wrap. Heat in microwave oven on Defrost until most ice crystals are gone and mixture can be easily stirred. Then heat on High until mixture reaches 165°F on instant-read thermometer, stirring gently once during heating.

MINESTRONE WITH PESTO

A little pesto goes a long way to liven up this traditional Italian soup. Save time and money by making it ahead (see Tip).

ACTIVE TIME: 20 MINUTES · TOTAL TIME: 1 HOUR 20 MINUTES PLUS SOAKING BEANS
MAKES: 6 MAIN-DISH SERVINGS

8   OUNCES DRIED GREAT NORTHERN BEANS (1⅓ CUPS)

2   TABLESPOONS OLIVE OIL

3   CARROTS, PEELED AND CUT INTO ¼-INCH SLICES

2   STALKS CELERY, CUT INTO ¼-INCH THICK SLICES

1   LARGE (12 OUNCES) ONION, FINELY CHOPPED

2   OUNCES SLICED PANCETTA OR BACON, FINELY CHOPPED

1   POUND ALL-PURPOSE POTATOES, PEELED AND CHOPPED

2   MEDIUM (8 OUNCES EACH) ZUCCHINI, EACH CUT LENGTHWISE INTO QUARTERS, THEN CROSSWISE INTO ¼-INCH PIECES

½   MEDIUM (1 POUND) HEAD SAVOY CABBAGE, SLICED TO EQUAL 4 CUPS

1 LARGE GARLIC CLOVE, CRUSHED WITH GARLIC PRESS

1 CAN (14½ OUNCES) DICED TOMATOES

2 CANS (14 TO 14½ OUNCES EACH) CHICKEN BROTH OR 3½ CUPS CHICKEN BROTH (PAGE 108)

1 CUP WATER

PESTO (OPPOSITE) OR ½ CUP PREPARED PESTO

½ TEASPOON SALT

1   Rinse beans under cold water and discard any stones or shriveled beans. In large bowl, place beans and 6 *cups water*; allow to stand at room temperature overnight. (Or, in 4-quart saucepan over high heat, heat beans and 6 *cups water* to boiling; cook 2 minutes. Remove from heat; cover and let stand 1 hour.) Drain and rinse beans.

2   In 4-quart saucepan, combine beans and enough *water* to cover by 2 inches; heat to boiling over high heat. Reduce heat; cover and simmer, stirring occasionally, until beans are tender, 40 minutes to 1 hour. Drain beans.

3   Meanwhile, in 5-quart Dutch oven, heat oil over medium-high heat. Add carrots, celery, onion, and pancetta; cook 10 minutes or until onions begin to brown, stirring occasionally.

4   Add potatoes, zucchini, cabbage, and garlic; cook, stirring constantly, until cabbage wilts. Add chicken broth, tomatoes with their juice, and 1 cup water; heat to boiling over high heat. Reduce heat to low; cover and simmer 30 minutes or until vegetables are tender.

5   Meanwhile, prepare pesto.

6 In blender or food processor with knife blade attached, blend ½ cup beans with 1 cup soup until pureed. Stir salt, bean puree, and remaining beans into soup; heat to boiling. Reduce heat to low; cover and simmer 10 minutes. Garnish with dollops of pesto.

PESTO

In blender at high speed, blend ⅔ **cup packed fresh basil leaves, ¼ cup grated Parmesan cheese, ¼ cup olive oil, 1 tablespoon water, and ¼ teaspoon salt** until smooth.

EACH SERVING WITH PESTO: ABOUT 425 CALORIES | 16G PROTEIN | 45G CARBOHYDRATE 22G TOTAL FAT (5G SATURATED) | 0G FIBER | 17MG CHOLESTEROL | 995MG SODIUM

TIP During the summer, when basil is plentiful and well priced, make up a double or triple batch of our homemade pesto. Pack it into a jar, top it off with a thin layer of olive oil to keep it nice and green, then put the lid on. Refrigerate for up to several months.

FRENCH ONION SOUP

Slowly cooked onions add great, caramelized flavor to this classic. A big salad completes the meal.

ACTIVE TIME: 1 HOUR · TOTAL TIME: 1 HOUR 50 MINUTES
MAKES: 4 MAIN-DISH SERVINGS

---

3   TABLESPOONS BUTTER OR MARGARINE

7   MEDIUM ONIONS (2½ POUNDS), EACH CUT LENGTHWISE IN HALF AND THINLY SLICED

¼   TEASPOON SALT

4   CUPS WATER

1   CAN (14 TO 14½ OUNCES) VEGETABLE BROTH (1¾ CUPS)

¼   TEASPOON DRIED THYME

4   SLICES (½-INCH THICK) FRENCH BREAD

4   OUNCES GRUYÈRE OR SWISS CHEESE, SHREDDED (1 CUP)

1   In 12-inch skillet, melt butter over medium heat. Add onions and salt and cook, stirring occasionally, until onions are very tender and beginning to caramelize, about 45 minutes. Reduce heat to low; cook, stirring often, until onions are deep golden brown, about 15 minutes longer.

2   Transfer onions to 3-quart saucepan. Add ½ cup water to skillet; heat to boiling over high heat, stirring until browned bits are loosened from bottom of pan. Pour into saucepan with onions. Add broth, thyme, and remaining water; heat to boiling over high heat. Reduce heat to low; cover and simmer until onions are very tender, about 30 minutes.

3   Meanwhile, preheat oven to 450°F. Place bread slices on small cookie sheet; bake until lightly toasted, about 5 minutes.

4   Place four 2½-cup oven-safe bowls in 15½" by 10½" jelly-roll pan. Spoon onion soup into bowls; top with toasted bread, pressing toast lightly into soup. Sprinkle toast with cheese. Bake until cheese melts and begins to brown, 12 to 15 minutes.

EACH SERVING: ABOUT 375 CALORIES | 15G PROTEIN | 38G CARBOHYDRATE | 23G TOTAL FAT (11G SATURATED) | 6G FIBER | 54MG CHOLESTEROL | 808MG SODIUM

BEEF-BARLEY AND ROOT VEGETABLE STEW

This stew is a delicious rib-sticker, hearty with parsnips, carrots, and mushrooms, as well as the barley and beef. Perfect for a cold winter night.

ACTIVE TIME: 25 MINUTES · TOTAL TIME: 2 HOURS 55 MINUTES

MAKES: 12 MAIN-DISH SERVINGS

---

2   SLICES BACON, CUT INTO ¼-INCH PIECES

3   POUNDS BONE-IN BEEF CHUCK STEAK

2   TEASPOONS PLUS 1 TABLESPOON VEGETABLE OIL

4   LARGE STALKS CELERY (12 OUNCES), CUT INTO ½-INCH-THICK SLICES

2   MEDIUM CARROTS, PEELED AND CUT INTO ½-INCH-THICK SLICES

2   SMALL PARSNIPS, PEELED AND CUT INTO ½-INCH-THICK SLICES

1   LARGE ONION, CHOPPED

1   PACKAGE (10 OUNCES) MUSHROOMS, TRIMMED AND EACH CUT INTO QUARTERS, OR EIGHTHS IF LARGE

3   TABLESPOONS TOMATO PASTE

12 CUPS WATER

2   TABLESPOONS SOY SAUCE

1   TABLESPOON SALT

1   PACKAGE (16 OUNCES) PEARL BARLEY, PICKED OVER, RINSED, AND DRAINED

1   In 6- to 8-quart saucepot, cook bacon over medium heat until browned, about 5 minutes. With slotted spoon, transfer bacon to medium bowl.

2   Meanwhile, trim and discard fat from beef. Cut beef into 1-inch chunks, reserving bones.

3   Add beef and bones, in 4 batches, to bacon drippings, and cook over medium-high heat until well browned on all sides, 3 to 4 minutes per batch, adding 2 teaspoons oil as necessary. (You may need to reduce heat to medium if drippings in saucepot begin to smoke.) With slotted spoon, transfer beef as it browns to bowl with bacon.

4   Reduce heat to medium. Add remaining 1 tablespoon oil to saucepot. Add celery, carrots, parsnips, onion, and mushrooms, and cook, covered, until vegetables are tender, 15 minutes, stirring occasionally. Add tomato paste and cook 1 minute, stirring.

5   Return meat with its juices and bacon to saucepot. Stir in water, soy sauce, and salt; heat to boiling over high heat. Reduce to low and simmer, covered, 45 minutes, stirring occasionally.

6   Stir in barley; heat to boiling over high heat. Reduce heat to low and simmer, covered, until beef and barley are tender, about 40 minutes longer, stirring occasionally.

EACH SERVING: ABOUT 305 CALORIES | 18G PROTEIN | 37G CARBOHYDRATE | 10G TOTAL FAT (3G SATURATED) | 8G FIBER | 47MG CHOLESTEROL | 898MG SODIUM

TURKEY AND WHITE BEAN CHILI

We love chili made with ground turkey (or even chicken); it is much lighter—and more healthful—than beef versions but just as flavorful.

TOTAL TIME: 20 MINUTES

MAKES: 4 MAIN-DISH SERVINGS

---

1 TABLESPOON OLIVE OIL

1 MEDIUM ONION, CHOPPED

1 POUND GROUND TURKEY

2 TEASPOONS GROUND CORIANDER

2 TEASPOONS GROUND CUMIN

2 TEASPOONS FRESH THYME LEAVES

2 CANS (15 TO 19 OUNCES EACH) GREAT NORTHERN BEANS, RINSED AND DRAINED

1 CAN (4 TO 4½ OUNCES) CHOPPED MILD GREEN CHILES

1 CAN (14 TO 14½ OUNCES) CHICKEN BROTH OR 1¾ CUPS CHICKEN BROTH (PAGE 108)

2 SMALL TOMATOES (4 OUNCES EACH), COARSELY CHOPPED

1 LIME, CUT INTO WEDGES

1 In nonstick 12-inch skillet, heat oil over medium-high heat until hot. Add onion and cook 5 minutes or until tender and golden, stirring frequently. Add turkey and cook 5 minutes or until it loses its pink color throughout, breaking up turkey with side of spoon. Stir in coriander, cumin, and thyme; cook 1 minute.

2 Meanwhile, in small bowl, mash half of beans.

3 Stir all beans, undrained chiles, and chicken broth into turkey mixture; heat to boiling over medium-high heat. Boil 1 minute or until chili thickens slightly. Stir in tomatoes. Serve with lime wedges.

EACH SERVING: ABOUT 495 CALORIES | 35G PROTEIN | 49G CARBOHYDRATE | 18G TOTAL FAT (4G SATURATED) | 17G FIBER | 90MG CHOLESTEROL | 1,040MG SODIUM

CARIBBEAN BLACK-BEAN SOUP

Black-bean soup is good news for your grocery bill. This version is made with sweet potatoes and fresh cilantro for great flavor.

ACTIVE TIME: 30 MINUTES · **TOTAL TIME:** 2 HOURS 30 MINUTES PLUS SOAKING BEANS
MAKES: 6 MAIN-DISH SERVINGS

- 1 PACKAGE (16 OUNCES) DRY BLACK BEANS
- 2 TABLESPOONS VEGETABLE OIL
- 2 MEDIUM RED ONIONS, CHOPPED
- 4 JALAPEÑO CHILES, SEEDED AND MINCED
- 2 TABLESPOONS MINCED, PEELED FRESH GINGER
- 4 GARLIC CLOVES, MINCED
- ½ TEASPOON GROUND ALLSPICE
- ½ TEASPOON DRIED THYME

- 8 CUPS WATER
- 2 MEDIUM SWEET POTATOES (1½ POUNDS) PEELED AND CUT INTO ¾-INCH PIECES
- 1 TABLESPOON DARK BROWN SUGAR
- 2 TEASPOONS SALT
- 1 BUNCH GREEN ONIONS, THINLY SLICED
- 1 CUP LIGHTLY PACKED FRESH CILANTRO, CHOPPED (OPTIONAL)
- 2 LIMES, CUT INTO WEDGES (OPTIONAL)

---

1 Rinse beans with cold running water and discard any stones or shriveled beans. In large bowl, place beans and enough *water* to cover by 2 inches. Cover and let stand at room temperature overnight. (Or, in 6-quart saucepot, heat beans and enough *water* to cover by 2 inches to boiling over high heat; cook 2 minutes. Remove from heat; cover and let stand 1 hour.) Drain and rinse beans.

2 In 6-quart saucepot, heat oil over medium heat until hot. Add onions and cook, stirring occasionally, until tender, about 10 minutes. Add jalapeños, ginger, garlic, allspice, and thyme; cook, stirring, 3 minutes.

3 Add beans and water; heat to boiling over high heat. Reduce heat to low; cover and simmer 1 hour 30 minutes.

4 Add sweet potatoes, brown sugar, and salt; heat to boiling over high heat. Reduce heat to low; cover and simmer until beans and sweet potatoes are tender, about 30 minutes longer.

5 Transfer 1 cup bean mixture to blender; cover, with center part of lid removed to let steam escape, and puree until smooth. Return puree to saucepot. Stir in green onions and cilantro. Serve with lime wedges, if you like.

EACH SERVING: ABOUT 390 CALORIES | 17G PROTEIN | 70G CARBOHYDRATE | 6G TOTAL FAT (1G SATURATED) | 19G FIBER | 0MG CHOLESTEROL | 705MG SODIUM

WINTER VEGETABLE CHOWDER

Clam isn't the only chowder in town. This version is packed with hearty vegetables and seasoned with a little bacon.

ACTIVE TIME: 40 MINUTES · TOTAL TIME: 50 MINUTES
MAKES: 6 MAIN-DISH SERVINGS

2 MEDIUM LEEKS (ABOUT 8 OUNCES)	2 CANS (14 TO 14½ OUNCES EACH) VEGETABLE OR CHICKEN BROTH OR 3½ CUPS CHICKEN BROTH (PAGE 108)
3 SLICES BACON, CUT INTO ½-INCH PIECES	
2 LARGE ALL-PURPOSE POTATOES (1½ POUNDS)	½ TEASPOON DRIED THYME
	½ TEASPOON SALT
1 LARGE CELERY ROOT (1½ POUNDS)	⅛ TEASPOON GROUND BLACK PEPPER
1 MEDIUM BUTTERNUT SQUASH (2¼ POUNDS)	1 CUP HALF-AND-HALF OR LIGHT CREAM

1 Cut off roots and trim dark green tops from leeks; cut each leek lengthwise in half, then crosswise into ¾-inch slices. Rinse leeks in large bowl of cold water, swishing to remove sand; transfer to colander to drain, leaving sand in bottom of bowl.

2 In 12-inch skillet, cook leeks and bacon over medium-high heat 7 to 10 minutes or until browned, stirring occasionally. Meanwhile, peel potatoes and cut into ½-inch chunks. Trim and peel celery root; cut into ½-inch chunks. Cut squash lengthwise in half; discard seeds. Remove peel and cut squash into 1-inch chunks.

3 Place potatoes, celery root, and squash in 4½- to 6-quart slow cooker. Stir in broth, thyme, salt, pepper, leek mixture, and *1 cup water*. Cover slow cooker with lid and cook on low setting as manufacturer directs, 7 to 8 hours or until all vegetables are very tender.

4 With slotted spoon, transfer about 2 cups cooked vegetables to small bowl. With potato masher, pastry blender, or fork, coarsely mash vegetables. Stir mashed vegetables back into slow cooker, then stir in half-and-half; heat through on high setting, if necessary.

EACH SERVING: ABOUT 380 CALORIES | 9G PROTEIN | 55G CARBOHYDRATE | 17G TOTAL FAT (7G SATURATED) | 6G FIBER | 27MG CHOLESTEROL | 1,047MG SODIUM

WALLET-FRIENDLY TIPS: BUYING AND STORING POTATOES

Select potatoes individually, choosing ones that are fairly clean, firm, and smooth. Avoid any with wrinkled or wilted skins, bruises, discolorations, or sprouts. Knobby potatoes and those with irregular shapes are more difficult to peel and produce more waste.

Reject potatoes with green-tinged skins, indicating prolonged exposure to light and the presence of solanine, which is a naturally occurring toxin. If greening is present, pare it away before cooking.

Store potatoes in a cool (45° to 50°F), humid (but not wet), dark, well-ventilated area. Never store potatoes in a refrigerator or below 40°F. Their starch will convert to sugar, and they will taste sweet. Check potatoes frequently and discard any that are badly shriveled or softened—one bad potato can adversely affect the remaining ones.

Do not wash potatoes ahead of time; it shortens storage life. Gently scrub them with a vegetable brush just before using them.

NEW ENGLAND COD CHOWDER

For a lower-fat take on a fishshack classic, try this winter warmer made with potatoes, fennel, carrots, and chunks of codfish.

ACTIVE TIME: 30 MINUTES · TOTAL TIME: 50 MINUTES
MAKES: 5 MAIN-DISH SERVINGS

---

4   SLICES BACON

3   MEDIUM CARROTS, EACH CUT LENGTHWISE IN HALF, THEN CROSSWISE INTO SLICES

1   LARGE (1 POUND) FENNEL BULB OR 3 CELERY STALKS, DICED

1   MEDIUM ONION, DICED

3   MEDIUM (1 POUND) ALL-PURPOSE POTATOES, PEELED AND CUT INTO ½-INCH CUBES

3   BOTTLES (8 OUNCES EACH) CLAM JUICE

1   CAN (14½-OUNCES) CHICKEN BROTH OR 1¾ CUPS CHICKEN BROTH (PAGE 108)

1   BAY LEAF

1   COD FILLET (1 POUND), CUT INTO 1½-INCH PIECES

1   CUP HALF-AND-HALF OR LIGHT CREAM

1   In 5-quart Dutch oven or saucepot, cook bacon over medium heat until browned. Remove bacon to paper towels to drain; crumble.

2   Discard all but 2 tablespoons bacon fat in Dutch oven. Add carrots, fennel, and onion, and cook until lightly browned, 6 to 8 minutes, stirring occasionally. Add potatoes, clam juice, chicken broth, and bay leaf; heat to boiling. Reduce heat to low; cover and simmer 10 to 15 minutes until vegetables are tender.

3   Add cod; cook, covered, 2 to 5 minutes until fish flakes easily when tested with a fork. Carefully stir in half-and-half; heat through. Discard bay leaf. Serve soup with crumbled bacon.

EACH SERVING: ABOUT 370 CALORIES | 25G PROTEIN | 36G CARBOHYDRATE | 14G TOTAL FAT (6G SATURATED) | 6G FIBER | 72MG CHOLESTEROL | 805MG SODIUM

BROCCOLI AND CHEDDAR SOUP

Served with homemade multigrain bread (or a bakery loaf) this rich soup makes a satisfying meal. Use a blender, not a food processor, for an extra-smooth texture.

ACTIVE TIME: 50 MINUTES · **TOTAL TIME:** 1 HOUR

MAKES: 4 MAIN-DISH SERVINGS

- 1 TABLESPOON OLIVE OIL
- 1 MEDIUM ONION, CHOPPED
- ¼ CUP ALL-PURPOSE FLOUR
- ½ TEASPOON SALT
- ¼ TEASPOON DRIED THYME
- ⅛ TEASPOON GROUND NUTMEG
- COARSELY GROUND BLACK PEPPER
- 2 CUPS REDUCED-FAT MILK (2%)

- 1 CAN (14 OUNCES) CHICKEN BROTH OR 1½ CUPS CHICKEN BROTH (PAGE 108)
- 1½ CUPS WATER
- 1 LARGE BUNCH BROCCOLI (1½ POUNDS), CUT INTO 1-INCH PIECES (INCLUDING STEMS)
- 1½ CUPS SHREDDED SHARP CHEDDAR CHEESE (6 OUNCES)

1   In 4-quart saucepan, heat oil over medium heat until hot. Add onion and cook, stirring occasionally, until golden, about 10 minutes. Stir in flour, salt, thyme, nutmeg, and ¼ teaspoon pepper; cook, stirring frequently, 2 minutes.

2   Gradually stir in milk, broth, and water. Add broccoli and heat to boiling over high heat. Reduce heat to low; cover and simmer until broccoli is tender, about 10 minutes.

3   Spoon one-third of mixture into blender; cover, with center part of lid removed to let steam escape, and puree until very smooth. Pour into large bowl. Repeat twice more with remaining mixture.

4   Return puree to same clean saucepan and heat to boiling over high heat, stirring occasionally. Remove from heat; stir in cheese until melted and smooth. To serve, sprinkle with coarsely ground black pepper.

EACH SERVING: ABOUT 364 CALORIES | 24G PROTEIN | 24G CARBOHYDRATE | 22G TOTAL FAT (12G SATURATED) | 5G FIBER | 5MG CHOLESTEROL | 972MG SODIUM

SPRING RAMEN CHICKEN SOUP

Ramen noodles are a staple for diners on a budget—and for good reason. Dress them up to create this flavorful Asian-style chicken noodle soup.

TOTAL TIME: 20 MINUTES

MAKES: 4 MAIN-DISH SERVINGS

5 CUPS WATER

2 PACKAGES (3 OUNCES EACH) CHICKEN-FLAVOR OR ORIENTAL-FLAVOR RAMEN NOODLE SOUP MIX

6 OUNCES SNOW PEAS (ABOUT 2 CUPS)

2 GREEN ONIONS

1 LARGE CARROT

1 POUND SKINLESS, BONELESS CHICKEN BREASTS

1 TEASPOON ASIAN SESAME OIL

1 In 4-quart saucepan, heat water with seasoning packets from ramen soup mix to boiling over high heat. Meanwhile, remove strings from snow peas and cut each diagonally in half. Slice green onions and shred carrot. Cut chicken into ¾-inch pieces. Break ramen noodle block into 2 layers.

2 When water mixture boils, add snow peas, green onions, carrot, chicken, and noodles. Cook 3 to 5 minutes over high heat or until chicken just loses its pink color throughout. Remove saucepan from heat. Stir in sesame oil.

EACH SERVING: ABOUT 355 CALORIES | 32G PROTEIN | 32G CARBOHYDRATE | 11G TOTAL FAT (4G SATURATED) | 3G FIBER | 66MG CHOLESTEROL | 920MG SODIUM

STRATEGY 7:
SUPPER IN A SALAD BOWL

Salad, in its most familiar guise, is a cool, crisp, refreshing collection of greens and vegetables tossed with a piquant dressing. But don't relegate salad to a supporting role: make it your main dish. Pasta, grains, beans and legumes, eggs, chicken, tuna, and even bread can all form wholesome—and economical—foundations for delicious main-dish salads that deserve a place of pride on your dinner table.

The best salads—from our classic Salad Niçoise to our Warm Lentil Salad with Shrimp, Apple, and Mint—contrast and balance textures, colors, and flavors. Crunchy and soft ingredients, tangy flavors with slightly sweet or mild ones, and bright colors combined with muted ones create salads that are pleasing to both the eyes and the taste buds. From composed and chopped salads to pasta, bean, and grain salads, all of our offerings do just that. And never think salad is only for summertime: chilled salads are perfect warm-weather meals to be sure, but we've included recipes for warm salads, too, which offer a welcome change of pace during the cooler months. We hope this fresh and wholesome collection of recipes will encourage you to make supper in a salad bowl one of your budget-dinner strategies.

Summer Cobb Salad with Lemon-Chive Dressing (page 130)

SALAD NIÇOISE

This classic French salad is composed of affordable ingredients, including canned tuna, green beans, and hard-boiled eggs.

ACTIVE TIME: 40 MINUTES · **TOTAL TIME:** 55 MINUTES
MAKES: 6 MAIN-DISH SERVINGS

PARSLEY VINAIGRETTE

¼ CUP LOOSELY PACKED FRESH PARSLEY LEAVES, CHOPPED

¼ CUP RED WINE VINEGAR

3 TABLESPOONS OLIVE OIL

1 TEASPOON DIJON MUSTARD

¼ TEASPOON SALT

¼ TEASPOON GROUND BLACK PEPPER

SALAD

1 POUND SMALL RED POTATOES, UNPEELED

6 LARGE EGGS

½ POUND GREEN BEANS, TRIMMED AND EACH CUT CROSSWISE IN HALF

1 HEAD BOSTON LETTUCE, SEPARATED INTO LEAVES (8 CUPS)

½ ENGLISH (SEEDLESS) CUCUMBER, THINLY SLICED

1 CAN (12 OUNCES) SOLID WHITE TUNA IN WATER, DRAINED

3 MEDIUM TOMATOES, CUT INTO WEDGES

½ CUP NIÇOISE OLIVES (3 OUNCES)

1 Prepare Parsley Vinaigrette: Into small bowl, measure vinaigrette ingredients. Mix with wire whisk or fork until well blended; set aside.

2 Prepare Salad: In 3-quart saucepan, place potatoes and enough *water* to cover; heat to boiling over high heat. Reduce heat to low; simmer 10 to 12 minutes or until potatoes are fork-tender.

3 Meanwhile, in 2-quart saucepan, place eggs and enough cold *water* to cover by 1 inch; heat to boiling over high heat. Immediately remove saucepan from heat and cover tightly; let stand 15 minutes. Pour off hot water; run cold water over eggs to cool. Remove shells and cut each egg into wedges.

4 When potatoes are done, with slotted spoon, remove potatoes from water to colander to drain. To same water in saucepan, add beans; heat to boiling over high heat. Reduce heat to low; simmer 5 to 10 minutes or until tender-crisp. Drain beans; rinse with cold running water to stop cooking; drain again.

5 In large bowl, toss greens with half of vinaigrette. Place greens on large platter. Cut each potato in half or into quarters if large; transfer to platter with greens. Arrange beans, eggs, cucumber, tuna, tomatoes, and olives in separate piles on same platter; drizzle with remaining vinaigrette.

EACH SERVING: ABOUT 315 CALORIES | 22G PROTEIN | 24G CARBOHYDRATE | 15G TOTAL FAT (3G SATURATED) | 4G FIBER | 233MG CHOLESTEROL | 515 MG SODIUM

CURRIED EGG SALAD ON GREENS

Served on greens, this classic Indian-spiced salad is a tasty dinner.

TOTAL TIME: 30 MINUTES
MAKES: 4 MAIN-DISH SERVINGS

6 LARGE EGGS	½ TEASPOON CURRY POWDER
1 TABLESPOON OLIVE OIL	2 STALKS CELERY, SLICED
1 LARGE ONION, SLICED	¼ CUP (LOOSELY PACKED) FRESH PARSLEY LEAVES, CHOPPED (OPTIONAL)
1 CUP FROZEN PEAS, THAWED	
¾ TEASPOON SALT	1 HEAD BOSTON LETTUCE, RINSED, DRAINED, AND TORN INTO 2-INCH PIECES
¼ TEASPOON COARSELY GROUND BLACK PEPPER	
1 LEMON	½ CUP WALNUTS, TOASTED AND CHOPPED
¼ CUP LIGHT MAYONNAISE	

1 Hard cook eggs: Place eggs in 3-quart saucepan with enough *water* to cover by 1 inch. Heat water, just to boiling, on high; remove from heat. Cover saucepan and let eggs stand 15 minutes.

2 While eggs are cooking, in 12-inch nonstick skillet, heat oil on medium 1 minute. Add onion and cook about 20 minutes or until very tender and golden-brown, stirring occasionally. Stir in peas, salt, and pepper; cook 3 minutes longer, until peas are cooked. Remove skillet from heat.

3 When eggs are done, carefully pour off water and cool eggs in same pan in cold water, changing water occasionally, until eggs are easy to handle, about 5 minutes. Meanwhile, from lemon, grate 1 teaspoon peel and squeeze 2 tablespoons juice. In small bowl, stir lemon peel and juice with mayonnaise and curry powder.

4 Remove shells from hard-cooked eggs. Coarsely chop eggs and place in large bowl. Add onion mixture, mayonnaise mixture, celery, and parsley, if using; stir gently with rubber spatula to combine. If you like, cover and refrigerate egg salad 1 hour or until chilled.

5 To serve, place lettuce on four dinner plates; top with egg salad and sprinkle with chopped walnuts.

EACH SERVING: ABOUT 355 CALORIES | 15G PROTEIN | 16G CARBOHYDRATE | 27G TOTAL FAT (5G SATURATED) | 5G FIBER | 323MG CHOLESTEROL | 715MG SODIUM

SWEET AND SAVORY COUSCOUS SALAD

This grain and green salad gets its citrusy sparkle from orange juice concentrate. None in your freezer? Use half regular orange juice and half lemon juice.

TOTAL TIME: 25 MINUTES
MAKES: 4 MAIN-DISH SERVINGS

- 1 CUP COUSCOUS (MOROCCAN PASTA)
- 1 CAN (14 TO 14½ OUNCES) VEGETABLE BROTH
- 3 TABLESPOONS OLIVE OIL
- ¼ CUP FROZEN ORANGE-JUICE CONCENTRATE, THAWED
- ¼ CUP BALSAMIC VINEGAR
- 1 TABLESPOON DIJON MUSTARD
- ½ TEASPOON SALT
- ¼ TEASPOON COARSELY GROUND BLACK PEPPER

- 2 TABLESPOONS WATER
- 1 CAN (15 TO 19 OUNCES) GARBANZO BEANS, RINSED AND DRAINED
- 3 GREEN ONIONS, CHOPPED
- ½ CUP PITTED PRUNES, CHOPPED
- 1 SMALL BUNCH (8 OUNCES) SPINACH, TOUGH STEMS TRIMMED
- 2 LARGE NAVEL ORANGES
- ¼ CUP SLICED ALMONDS, TOASTED

1 Prepare couscous as label directs but use broth plus *water* to equal amount of water called for on label, and do not use butter or margarine or salt.

2 In large bowl, with wire whisk or fork, mix oil, orange-juice concentrate, vinegar, mustard, salt, pepper, and water. Stir in couscous, garbanzo beans, green onions, and prunes; toss well.

3 Reserve several small spinach leaves for garnish. Tear remaining leaves into bite-size pieces and stir into couscous mixture. Cut peel and white pith from both oranges. Cut 1 orange into slices; cut each slice in half. Cut remaining orange into bite-size chunks. Stir orange chunks into couscous mixture.

4 Spoon couscous salad into large bowl. Garnish with orange slices and reserved spinach leaves. Sprinkle almonds on top.

EACH SERVING: ABOUT 600 CALORIES | 16G PROTEIN | 100G CARBOHYDRATE | 15G TOTAL FAT (2G SATURATED) | 13G FIBER | 0MG CHOLESTEROL | 1,010MG SODIUM

SUMMER COBB SALAD WITH LEMON-CHIVE DRESSING

Hot, sunny evenings call for a simple menu made with minimal effort. This lightened-up take on cobb salad uses corn, honeydew, and roasted turkey breast—a colorful, healthy combo for the summer season.

TOTAL TIME: 20 MINUTES

MAKES: 6 MAIN-DISH SERVINGS

- 4 SLICES BACON
- ⅓ CUP FRESH LEMON JUICE
- 2 TEASPOONS DIJON MUSTARD
- ½ TEASPOON SALT
- ¼ TEASPOON COARSELY GROUND BLACK PEPPER
- ⅓ CUP OLIVE OIL
- ¼ CUP SNIPPED FRESH CHIVES PLUS ADDITIONAL FOR GARNISH (OPTIONAL)
- 1 LARGE HEAD ROMAINE LETTUCE (1¼ POUNDS), CUT INTO ¾-INCH PIECES (10 CUPS)
- 12 OUNCES ROASTED BONELESS TURKEY BREAST IN 1 PIECE, SKIN DISCARDED, CUT INTO ½-INCH CHUNKS (SEE TIP)
- 1½ CUPS FRESH CORN KERNELS (FROM 3 TO 4 EARS)
- ¼ HONEYDEW MELON (1¼ POUNDS), CUT INTO ½-INCH CHUNKS (3 CUPS)
- 4 OUNCES FETA OR GOAT CHEESE, CRUMBLED (1 CUP)
- 1 RIPE AVOCADO, PEELED AND CUT INTO ½-INCH CHUNKS

1 In small skillet, cook bacon on medium until browned, about 8 minutes. Transfer bacon to paper towels to drain; crumble when cool.

2 Meanwhile, prepare dressing: In small bowl, with wire whisk, mix lemon juice, Dijon, salt, and pepper. In thin, steady stream, whisk in oil until blended. Stir in snipped chives, if using.

3 Line large platter with romaine. Arrange bacon, turkey, corn, melon, feta cheese, and avocado in rows over romaine. Garnish salad with chives, if you like. Serve with dressing.

TIP When shopping for turkey breast in your deli, ask for a piece cut from a whole store-roasted breast instead of the pressed deli-meat variety that's typically quite salty and often filled with preservatives.

EACH SERVING: ABOUT 425 CALORIES | 27G PROTEIN | 25G CARBOHYDRATE | 26G TOTAL FAT (7G SATURATED) | 5G FIBER | 66MG CHOLESTEROL | 425MG SODIUM

WALLET-FRIENDLY GUIDE: OLIVE OILS

Extra virgin, the highest grade and the most expensive of olive oils, is also the least acidic. It is extracted from olives in a cold-press process. Because of its superior taste (often described as intensely fruity) and aroma, it's best used at the end of cooking or just before serving to really enhance flavor. It's also wonderful in salad dressings.

Virgin olive oil is produced in the same manner as extra virgin but is more acidic. It's not widely available to consumers; most of the time it's blended with other oils before bottling.

Olive oil (formerly called "pure olive oil") is produced by refining and neutralizing virgin olive oil that doesn't meet international Olive Oil Council standards. The refined oil is then blended with up to 25 percent virgin or extra virgin oil to add characteristic flavor. This pale green or yellow all-purpose oil has a less pronounced flavor and aroma than extra virgin—it works well in simple dressings and sautés.

Light olive oil, which is filtered to remove some of olive oil's usual flavor, color, and fragrance, is not lower in calories or fat. But it's an excellent choice when you don't want the flavor of a full-bodied oil. It can also be used in place of vegetable oil in baking.

WARM LENTIL SALAD WITH SHRIMP, APPLE, AND MINT

This heart-healthy salad is chock-full of fiber thanks to a crisp Golden Delicious apple and a nutty lentil base.

ACTIVE TIME: 20 MINUTES · **TOTAL TIME:** 30 MINUTES
MAKES: 4 MAIN-DISH SERVINGS

---

3 TABLESPOONS OLIVE OIL	1 CUP LENTILS
3 TABLESPOONS CIDER VINEGAR	6 CUPS WATER
1½ TEASPOONS SALT	1 SMALL ONION, CHOPPED
¼ TEASPOON COARSELY GROUND BLACK PEPPER	½ CUP (LOOSELY PACKED) FRESH MINT LEAVES, CHOPPED
1 POUND FRESH OR FROZEN (THAWED) SHELLED AND DEVEINED MEDIUM SHRIMP	1 GOLDEN DELICIOUS APPLE, UNPEELED, CORED, AND CUT INTO ½-INCH CHUNKS
	1 STALK CELERY, THINLY SLICED

1 In small bowl, whisk oil, vinegar, salt, and pepper. Spoon 2 tablespoons dressing into medium bowl. Add shrimp; toss to coat.

2 In colander, rinse lentils with cold water, and discard any stones or shriveled lentils. In 4-quart saucepan, combine lentils, water, onion, and 2 tablespoons mint; heat to boiling on high. Reduce heat to low; cover and simmer 8 to 10 minutes or until lentils are tender but still hold their shape. Drain well.

3 Meanwhile, heat 12-inch skillet on medium-high until hot. Add shrimp with the 2 tablespoons dressing, and cook 4 to 5 minutes or until shrimp turn opaque. Remove from heat; stir in 1 tablespoon mint.

4 Stir shrimp, apple, celery, and remaining mint and dressing into lentils.

EACH SERVING: ABOUT 410 CALORIES | 37G PROTEIN | 37G CARBOHYDRATE | 13G TOTAL FAT (2G SATURATED) | 17G FIBER | 172MG CHOLESTEROL | 475MG SODIUM

BLACK BEAN AND AVOCADO SALAD WITH CILANTRO DRESSING

A satisfying combination of summer veggies, romaine lettuce, and black beans tossed with a creamy cilantro-lime dressing.

TOTAL TIME: 30 MINUTES

MAKES: 4 MAIN-DISH SERVINGS

CILANTRO DRESSING

2   LIMES

¼   CUP LIGHT MAYONNAISE

½   CUP PACKED FRESH CILANTRO LEAVES

2   TABLESPOONS REDUCED-FAT SOUR CREAM

½   TEASPOON GROUND CUMIN

¼   TEASPOON SUGAR

⅛   TEASPOON SALT

⅛   TEASPOON COARSELY GROUND BLACK PEPPER

SALAD

1   SMALL HEAD ROMAINE LETTUCE (1 POUND), CUT INTO ¾-INCH PIECES (8 CUPS)

2   MEDIUM TOMATOES, CUT INTO ½-INCH PIECES

2   KIRBY CUCUMBERS (4 OUNCES EACH), UNPEELED, EACH CUT LENGTHWISE INTO QUARTERS, THEN CROSSWISE INTO ¼-INCH-THICK PIECES

1   RIPE AVOCADO, PEELED AND CUT INTO ½-INCH PIECES

1   CAN (15 TO 19 OUNCES) BLACK BEANS, RINSED AND DRAINED

1 Prepare dressing: From limes, grate ½ teaspoon peel and squeeze 3 tablespoons juice. In blender, combine lime peel and juice, mayonnaise, cilantro, sour cream, cumin, sugar, salt, and pepper; puree, occasionally scraping down sides of blender, until smooth. Cover and refrigerate if not using right away. Makes about ½ cup.

2 Prepare salad: In large serving bowl, combine romaine, tomatoes, cucumbers, avocado, and beans. Add dressing and toss until evenly coated.

EACH SERVING: ABOUT 230 CALORIES | 9G PROTEIN | 34G CARBOHYDRATE | 10G TOTAL FAT (2G SATURATED) | 15G FIBER | 3MG CHOLESTEROL | 520MG SODIUM

SZECHUAN NOODLE PEANUT SALAD

A tasty pasta salad packed with great Asian flavors. To serve cold, chill the pasta and toss with the vegetables just before serving.

ACTIVE TIME: 20 MINUTES · **TOTAL TIME:** 30 MINUTES
MAKES: 5 MAIN-DISH SERVINGS

- 1 PACKAGE (16 OUNCES) LINGUINE OR SPAGHETTI
- 2½ TEASPOONS SALT
- 4 OUNCES SNOW PEAS, STRINGS REMOVED
- ½ CUP CREAMY PEANUT BUTTER
- 1 TABLESPOON GRATED, PEELED FRESH GINGER
- ¼ CUP SOY SAUCE
- 2 TABLESPOONS DISTILLED WHITE VINEGAR
- 2 TEASPOONS ASIAN SESAME OIL
- ¼ TEASPOON HOT PEPPER SAUCE
- 1 SMALL CUCUMBER (6 OUNCES), PEELED, SEEDED, AND CUT INTO 2-INCH-BY-¼-INCH MATCHSTICK STRIPS
- ¼ CUP DRY-ROASTED PEANUTS
- 1 GREEN ONION, TRIMMED AND CHOPPED

1 In large saucepot, cook linguine as label directs, using 2 teaspoons salt.

2 Meanwhile, in 3-quart saucepan, heat *1 inch water* to boiling; add snow peas. Reduce heat and simmer 2 minutes; drain. Rinse with cold running water; drain. Cut snow peas lengthwise into ¼-inch-wide matchstick strips; set aside.

3 Drain linguine, reserving *1 cup pasta water.*

4 Prepare dressing: In large bowl, with wire whisk, mix peanut butter, ginger, reserved pasta water, soy sauce, vinegar, sesame oil, hot pepper sauce, and remaining ½ teaspoon salt until smooth.

5 Add linguine to dressing in bowl and toss to coat. Add snow peas and cucumber; toss to combine. Sprinkle with peanuts and green onion.

EACH SERVING: ABOUT 572 CALORIES | 22G PROTEIN | 78G CARBOHYDRATE | 20G TOTAL FAT (3G SATURATED) | 6G FIBER | 0G CHOLESTEROL | 1,794MG SODIUM

STRATEGY 8:
CHEAP GRILLS

Easy prep, cooking, and cleanup make grilling a popular dinnertime strategy, but anyone who does it regularly knows it is not always the thriftiest solution. Purchase enough ribs, strip steaks, or jumbo shrimp to satisfy your family and your carefully planned grocery budget may feel like it's been flayed, skewered, and charbroiled. But don't retire your favorite tongs and marinade; this chapter offers a variety of ways to grill up crowd-pleasing dinners on a you-pleasing budget.

First off, you need the right meat. Tougher cuts like flank steak and brisket do well on the grill, especially if they are marinated in a tangy sauce or thoroughly coated with a spicy rub. For the most affordable grilled chicken dinner, grill bone-in parts or a couple pounds of thighs instead of shelling out extra money for boneless skinless chicken breasts that will yield a less flavorful grill anyway. For more ways to save money, see our wallet-friendly tips for meat (page 139) and poultry (page 145).

And, of course, you can't forget the burgers. They're so easy and fun to grill, and even more fun to eat. To mix things up, consider alternating beef burgers with other tasty (and healthful) options, like chicken, turkey, and even bean burgers. Which reminds us: the grill is not just for meat—for a tasty and economical change of pace, check out our recipes with veggies, tofu, and tortillas all made in a jiffy on the grill.

Lemon Chicken with Grilled Summer Squash (page 146)

PASTRAMI-SPICED FLANK STEAK

Thinly sliced flank steak makes a perfect pastrami. Ours isn't smoked like the New York City deli favorite, but it is similarly coated with coarse pepper and other aromatic spices. For full effect, serve it on sliced rye with a side of coleslaw.

ACTIVE TIME: 15 MINUTES · **TOTAL TIME:** 30 MINUTES PLUS MARINATING
MAKES: 6 SERVINGS

---

1 TABLESPOON CORIANDER SEEDS	½ TEASPOON CRUSHED RED PEPPER
1 TABLESPOON PAPRIKA	3 GARLIC CLOVES, CRUSHED WITH GARLIC PRESS
1 TABLESPOON CRACKED BLACK PEPPER	
2 TEASPOONS GROUND GINGER	1 BEEF FLANK STEAK (1½ POUNDS), WELL TRIMMED
1½ TEASPOONS SALT	12 SLICES RYE BREAD
1 TEASPOON SUGAR	DELI-STYLE MUSTARD

1 In mortar with pestle (see Tip) or in zip-tight plastic bag with rolling pin, crush coriander seeds. In cup, mix coriander, paprika, black pepper, ginger, salt, sugar, and crushed red pepper.

2 Rub garlic on both sides of steak, then pat with spice mixture. Place steak in large zip-tight plastic bag; seal bag, pressing out excess air. Place bag on plate; refrigerate at least 2 hours, or up to 24 hours.

3 Prepare outdoor grill for direct grilling over medium heat.

4 Remove steak from bag. Place steak on hot grill rack over medium heat and grill, turning once, 13 to 15 minutes for medium-rare or until desired doneness.

5 Place bread slices on grill rack over medium heat and toast, without turning, just until grill marks appear on underside of bread.

6 Transfer steak to cutting board and let stand 10 minutes to allow juices to set for easier slicing. Thinly slice steak across the grain and serve with grilled rye bread and mustard.

TIP Grinding whole spices in a mortar with a pestle releases their flavorful oils, which makes the steak even tastier.

EACH SERVING: ABOUT 380 CALORIES | 33G PROTEIN | 35G CARBOHYDRATE | 12G TOTAL FAT (4G SATURATED) | 2G FIBER | 47MG CHOLESTEROL | 1,015MG SODIUM

WALLET-FRIENDLY TIPS: MEAT

Buy value cuts like chuck pot roast, beef brisket, and pork shoulder. While not as juicy or as quick-cooking as rib-eye or pork loin roasts, they have top-notch flavor, tenderize with slow-cooking, and can feed a crowd.

Skip those pricey premade burger patties. Make your own with ground beef from a family pack of three or more pounds and save nearly 15 cents per patty. Freeze any extra meat for another night.

Try a flat iron steak (also called "top blade") for an economical version of premium filet mignon for one-third of the cost. This newly created cut, from the steer's shoulder blade, used to go into the grinder for hamburger until a more precise cutting technique was developed.

TEX-MEX BURGERS

Everyone craves a good beef burger from time to time. For an all-out splurge, serve with shredded lettuce, sliced red onion, extra salsa, and guacamole. For a spicier burger, choose a medium to hot salsa and increase the chili powder to 2 teaspoons. Top the burger with sliced Monteray Jack, cover the grill to melt the cheese, and you've got a Tex-Mex cheeseburger.

ACTIVE TIME: 10 MINUTES · **TOTAL TIME:** 20 MINUTES
MAKES: 4 BURGERS

1	POUND LEAN GROUND BEEF (90%)	½	TEASPOON SALT
2	TABLESPOONS MINCED ONION	1	TEASPOON CHILI POWDER
2	TABLESPOONS BOTTLED SALSA	4	SEEDED ROLLS, SPLIT

1   Prepare outdoor grill for direct grilling over medium heat.

2   In medium bowl, combine ground beef, onion, salsa, salt, and chili powder just until well blended but not overmixed. Shape mixture into 4 patties, each 1 inch thick, handling meat as little as possible. (Gentle handling is one of the keys to juicy burgers. Use a light hand when shaping patties, so burgers won't come out compact and dry.)

3   Place burgers on hot grill rack over medium heat and grill, turning once, 10 to 12 minutes for medium or until desired doneness.

4   Place rolls, cut side down, on grill over medium heat and toast, without turning, just until grill marks appear on cut side of rolls. Serve burgers on rolls with toppings described above, if you like.

TIP The best ground beef for burgers has some fat in it (about 10% works nicely) for juiciness and flavor, so don't use the very leanest ground beef.

EACH BURGER: ABOUT 325 CALORIES | 27G PROTEIN | 23G CARBOHYDRATE | 14G TOTAL FAT (5G SATURATED) | 2G FIBER | 70MG CHOLESTEROL | 670MG SODIUM

CHICKEN BURGERS

If you're looking for plain, straightforward burgers, we've got them. We also have suggestions to jazz them up, so pick your favorite flavor family—teriyaki, barbecue, or herb.

ACTIVE TIME: 10 MINUTES · TOTAL TIME: 30 MINUTES
MAKES: 4 BURGERS

BASIC BURGERS

1 POUND GROUND CHICKEN BREASTS

1 MEDIUM CARROT, GRATED (½ CUP)

2 GREEN ONIONS, MINCED

1 CLOVE GARLIC, CRUSHED WITH GARLIC PRESS

4 HAMBURGER BUNS, WARMED

SLICED CUCUMBER, LETTUCE LEAVES, AND GREEN ONION (OPTIONAL)

1 Prepare Basic Burgers: In medium bowl, with hand, mix ground chicken, carrot, green onions, and garlic until evenly combined.

2 On waxed paper, shape chicken mixture into four 3½-inch round patties (mixture will be very soft and moist).

3 Place patties on grill over medium heat and cook, turning once, about 12 minutes or until juices run clear when center of burger is pierced with tip of knife. (If you have a grill with widely spaced grates, you may want to place burgers on a perforated grill topper to keep them intact.)

4 Place burgers on warmed buns. Serve with cucumber slices, lettuce leaves, and green onions, if you like.

EACH BURGER: ABOUT 295 CALORIES | 30G PROTEIN | 24G CARBOHYDRATE | 5G TOTAL FAT (1G SATURATED) | 2G FIBER | 72MG CHOLESTEROL | 310MG SODIUM

TERIYAKI BURGERS

Prepare and cook Chicken Burgers as directed, but in step 1, add **2 tablespoons soy sauce**; **1 tablespoon seasoned rice vinegar**; **2 teaspoons grated, peeled fresh ginger**; and **2 teaspoons Asian sesame oil** to ground chicken mixture. (Prepare burger mixture just before cooking to prevent ginger from changing texture of meat.)

EACH BURGER: ABOUT 305 CALORIES | 31G PROTEIN | 26G CARBOHYDRATE | 8G TOTAL FAT (2G SATURATED) | 2G FIBER | 72MG CHOLESTEROL | 940MG SODIUM

BARBECUE BURGERS

Prepare and cook Chicken Burgers as directed, but in step 1, add **2 table-spoons chili sauce, 1 tablespoon light (mild) molasses, 2 teaspoons cayenne pepper sauce, 2 teaspoons Worcestershire sauce,** and **¼ tea-spoon salt** to ground chicken mixture.

EACH BURGER: ABOUT 295 CALORIES | 31G PROTEIN | 30G CARBOHYDRATE | 5G TOTAL FAT (1G SATURATED) | 2G FIBER | 72MG CHOLESTEROL | 715 MG SODIUM

HERB BURGERS

Prepare and cook Chicken Burgers as directed but in step 1, add **2 table-spoons finely chopped fresh dill, 1 tablespoon dried mint, 1 tablespoon fresh lemon juice, 1 teaspoon ground cumin, ½ teaspoon salt,** and **⅛ teaspoon cayenne pepper** to ground chicken mixture.

EACH BURGER: ABOUT 280 CALORIES | 31G PROTEIN | 25G CARBOHYDRATE | 5G TOTAL FAT (1G SATURATED) | 2G FIBER | 72MG CHOLESTEROL | 605MG SODIUM

PEKING CHICKEN ROLL-UPS

The traditional Chinese recipe for duck is expensive and labor-intensive. Our version, prepared on the cheap and in minutes, is made with grilled boneless chicken thighs and served in flour tortillas with hoisin sauce.

ACTIVE TIME: 25 MINUTES · **TOTAL TIME:** 35 MINUTES
MAKES: 4 MAIN-DISH SERVINGS

8   (8-INCH) FLOUR TORTILLAS

2   TABLESPOONS HONEY

2   TABLESPOONS SOY SAUCE

1   TABLESPOON GRATED, PEELED FRESH GINGER

⅛   TEASPOON GROUND RED PEPPER (CAYENNE)

2   GARLIC CLOVES, CRUSHED WITH GARLIC PRESS

6   SKINLESS, BONELESS CHICKEN THIGHS (ABOUT 1¼ POUNDS)

1   TEASPOON VEGETABLE OIL

¼   CUP HOISIN SAUCE

½   ENGLISH (SEEDLESS) CUCUMBER, CUT INTO 2" BY ¼" STICKS

2   GREEN ONIONS, THINLY SLICED

1   Stack tortillas and wrap in foil. In small bowl, mix honey, soy sauce, ginger, ground red pepper, and garlic until blended. Set aside tortillas and honey mixture.

2   Coat chicken with oil and place on grill over medium-high heat. Cook 5 minutes, turning over once. Brush chicken all over with honey mixture, and cook 5 to 7 minutes longer or until juices run clear when thickest part of thigh is pierced with tip of knife, turning over once.

3   While chicken is cooking, place foil-wrapped tortillas on same grill, and heat 3 to 5 minutes or until warm.

4   Transfer chicken to cutting board and thinly slice. Spread hoisin sauce on one side of tortillas; top with chicken, cucumber, and green onions, and roll up to serve.

EACH SERVING: ABOUT 400 CALORIES │ 27G PROTEIN │ 50G CARBOHYDRATE │ 10G TOTAL FAT (3G SATURATED) │ 4G FIBER │ 75MG CHOLESTEROL │ 1,255MG SODIUM

WALLET-FRIENDLY TIPS: POULTRY

Supermarket rotisserie chicken makes a fast meal, but convenience will cost more. You can roast your own three-pounder in an hour with inexpensive herbs from the pantry for half the price.

Swap bone-in chicken thighs for boneless chicken breasts (when possible). You can buy almost three times as much for the same price. Plus thighs are perfect for easy prep-and-cook casseroles.

Not just for holidays, a hefty gobbler can serve up three hearty dinners with enough meat left over for sandwiches. Choose a frozen turkey, over fresh breast fillets, for one-fourth the price.

LEMON CHICKEN WITH GRILLED SUMMER SQUASH

For this easy summer supper, simply toss the sliced squash on the grill along with the marinated chicken. You can use zucchini, yellow squash, or a combination. (See page 136 for photo.)

TOTAL TIME: 25 MINUTES PLUS MARINATING

MAKES: 4 SERVINGS

---

1 LEMON

1 TABLESPOON OLIVE OIL

½ TEASPOON SALT

¼ TEASPOON COARSELY GROUND BLACK PEPPER

4 MEDIUM SKINLESS, BONELESS CHICKEN THIGHS (1¼ POUNDS)

4 MEDIUM YELLOW SUMMER SQUASH AND/OR ZUCCHINI (6 OUNCES EACH), EACH CUT LENGTHWISE INTO 4 WEDGES

¼ CUP SNIPPED FRESH CHIVES (OPTIONAL)

1 From lemon, grate 1 tablespoon peel and squeeze 3 tablespoons juice. In medium bowl, whisk together lemon peel and juice, oil, salt, and pepper; transfer 2 tablespoons marinade to cup and reserve.

2 Add chicken to bowl with lemon-juice marinade; toss until evenly coated. Cover and let stand 15 minutes at room temperature or 30 minutes in the refrigerator.

3 Meanwhile, prepare outdoor grill for covered direct grilling over medium heat.

4 Discard chicken marinade. Place chicken and squash on hot grill rack over medium heat. Cover grill and cook, turning chicken and squash over once and removing pieces as they are done, until juices run clear when thickest part of thigh is pierced with tip of knife and squash is tender and browned, 10 to 12 minutes.

5 Transfer chicken and squash to cutting board. Cut chicken into 1-inch-wide strips; cut each squash wedge crosswise in half.

6 To serve, on large platter, toss squash with reserved lemon-juice marinade, then toss with chicken and sprinkle with chives, if using.

EACH SERVING: ABOUT 255 CALORIES | 29G PROTEIN | 8G CARBOHYDRATE | 8G TOTAL FAT (3G SATURATED) | 2G FIBER | 101MG CHOLESTEROL | 240MG SODIUM

HOISIN-GINGER-GLAZED TOFU AND VEGGIES

Grilling isn't just for meat: for a delicious vegetarian medley, brush this hoisin-ginger glaze on tofu, zucchini, and red pepper. Be sure to buy extra-firm tofu; other varieties will fall apart while cooking.

TOTAL TIME: 30 MINUTES

MAKES: 4 MAIN-DISH SERVINGS

HOISIN-GINGER GLAZE

- ½ CUP HOISIN SAUCE
- 2 GARLIC CLOVES, CRUSHED WITH GARLIC PRESS
- 1 TABLESPOON VEGETABLE OIL
- 1 TABLESPOON REDUCED-SODIUM SOY SAUCE
- 1 TABLESPOON GRATED, PEELED FRESH GINGER
- 1 TABLESPOON SEASONED RICE VINEGAR
- ⅛ TEASPOON GROUND RED PEPPER (CAYENNE)

TOFU AND VEGGIES

- 1 PACKAGE (15 OUNCES) EXTRA-FIRM TOFU
- 2 MEDIUM ZUCCHINI (10 OUNCES EACH), EACH CUT LENGTHWISE INTO QUARTERS, THEN CROSSWISE IN HALF
- 1 LARGE RED PEPPER, STEM AND SEEDS REMOVED, CUT LENGTHWISE INTO QUARTERS
- 1 BUNCH GREEN ONIONS, TRIMMED
- 1 TEASPOON VEGETABLE OIL

---

1 Prepare outdoor grill for direct grilling over medium heat.

2 Prepare glaze: In small bowl, with fork, mix hoisin sauce, garlic, oil, soy sauce, ginger, vinegar, and ground red pepper until well blended.

3 Prepare tofu and veggies: Cut tofu horizontally into 4 pieces, then cut each piece crosswise in half. Place tofu on paper towels; pat dry with additional paper towels. Arrange tofu on large plate and brush both sides of tofu with half of glaze. Spoon remaining half of glaze into medium bowl; add zucchini and red pepper. Gently toss vegetables to coat with glaze. On another plate, rub green onions with oil.

4 Place tofu, zucchini, and red peppers on hot grill rack over medium heat and grill tofu, gently turning once with wide metal spatula, 6 minutes. Transfer tofu to platter; keep warm. Continue cooking vegetables, transferring them to platter with tofu as they are done, until tender and browned, about 5 minutes longer.

5 Add green onions to grill rack during last minute of cooking time; transfer to platter.

EACH SERVING: ABOUT 245 CALORIES | 15G PROTEIN | 22G CARBOHYDRATE | 11G TOTAL FAT (1G SATURATED) | 5G FIBER | 0MG CHOLESTEROL | 615MG SODIUM

GRILLED CORN AND JACK QUESADILLAS

These quesadillas make a fun and simple summertime meal. To save time, grate the cheese for the quesadillas while the corn is grilling.

ACTIVE TIME: 15 MINUTES · **TOTAL TIME:** 20 MINUTES PLUS COOLING

MAKES: 4 MAIN-DISH SERVINGS

---

3   LARGE EARS CORN, HUSKS AND SILK REMOVED

4   LOW-FAT BURRITO-SIZE (8- TO 10-INCH) FLOUR TORTILLAS

4   OUNCES REDUCED-FAT MONTEREY JACK CHEESE, SHREDDED (1 CUP)

½   CUP MILD OR MEDIUM-HOT SALSA

2   GREEN ONIONS, THINLY SLICED

1   Prepare outdoor grill for covered direct grilling over medium-high heat.

2   Place corn on hot grill rack over medium-high heat. Cover grill and cook corn, turning frequently, until brown in spots, 10 to 15 minutes.

3   Transfer corn to plate; set aside until cool enough to handle. When cool, with sharp knife, cut kernels from cobs.

4   Place tortillas on work surface. Evenly divide Monterey Jack, salsa, green onions, and corn on half of each tortilla. Fold tortilla over filling to make 4 quesadillas.

5   Place quesadillas on hot grill rack. Grill quesadillas, turning once, until browned on both sides, 1 to 2 minutes. Transfer to cutting board; cut each quesadilla into 3 pieces.

EACH SERVING: ABOUT 330 CALORIES | 16G PROTEIN | 47G CARBOHYDRATE | 11G TOTAL FAT (5G SATURATED) | 10G FIBER | 20MG CHOLESTEROL | 940MG SODIUM

WHAT CONVENIENCE COSTS

We wholeheartedly believe in making dinnertime easy. But before you fill your shopping cart with processed, prepackaged ingredients, take a look at what convenience costs you. One grocery bill might not be daunting, but consider how the savings would add up over a year if you choose cheap over convenient. (Costs are approximate, but the ratios are typical.)

CHEAP	CONVENIENT
CABBAGE, HEAD Green cabbage, 1 lb. at $.59/lb. $.10 per serving	**CABBAGE SHREDDED** $1.99/1 lb. bag coleslaw mix $.33 per serving
GROUND BEEF (85% LEAN) $3.69/lb. $.92 per 4-oz. patty	**BEEF PATTIES, PREMADE (85% LEAN)** $4.19/lb. $1.05 per 4-oz. patty
ROMAINE, HEAD $.99/lb. $.25 per serving	**ROMAINE, CUT** $3.49/10-oz. bag $.97 per serving
DRIED BEANS $.99/16 oz. red kidney $.10 per serving	**CANNED BEANS** $1.75/15.5 oz. red kidney $.25 per serving
BROCCOLI, BUNCH $1.99 each $.50 per serving	**BROCCOLI, FLORETS** $2.99/12-oz bag $.75 per serving
CARROTS, WHOLE $.99/lb. $.25 per serving	**CARROTS, SHREDDED** $1.69/10-oz. bag $.48 per serving

CHEAP	CONVENIENT
SPLIT CHICKEN BREASTS (BONE-IN) $2.99/lb. $.75 per serving	**CHICKEN CUTLETS (BONELESS)** $5.99/lb. $1.49 per serving
RUSSETS (BAKING POTATOES) $2.99/5-lb. bag $.20 per serving	**FROZEN STEAK FRIES** $3.89/28 oz. thick-cut steak fries $.43 per serving
MOZZARELLA CHEESE, BALL $5.69/16 oz. part-skim $.36 per serving	**MOZZARELLA CHEESE, SHREDDED** $3.49/8 oz. part-skim $.44 per serving
GREEN BEANS, FRESH $1.49/lb. $.37 per serving	**GREEN BEANS, FRESH MICROWAVE/STEAM-IN BAG** $3.99/12 oz. $1.33 per serving
WHOLE-GRAIN BROWN RICE, RAW, MICROWAVEABLE $1.89/16 oz. (30 min. cook time) $.19 per serving	**WHOLE-GRAIN BROWN RICE, POUCH (PRECOOKED)** $2.19/8.8 oz. (90 sec. cook time) $1.10 per serving
CELERY $2.29/2 lb. bunch $.29 per serving	**CELERY STICKS** $2.49/8 oz. $.62 per serving

HOW TO FREEZE ANYTHING

Maximize the longevity of your purchases by freezing them. To avoid freezer burn, leave as little extra air in the bag or container as possible. If you take a defrosting shortcut, like zapping edibles in the microwave instead of thawing them in the fridge, fully cook the food before refreezing.

	WHAT TO SAVE	IN FRIDGE (set at or below 40°F)	IN FREEZER	HOW TO STORE IN FREEZER (set at or below 0°F)
FRUIT	**Bananas, ripe**	2 weeks	8 to 12 months	In peel, in freezer bag (peel may discolor)
	Blackberries and Raspberries	2 to 3 days	8 to 12 months	Spread on tray and freeze until firm, then store in a sealed container or freezer bag
	Blueberries	10 days	8 to 12 months	In original container, placed in freezer bag
	Cranberries	4 weeks	8 to 12 months	In original bag (if unopened) or freezer bag
	Grapes	1 to 2 weeks	8 to 12 months	See Blackberries, above (remove from stems)
GRAINS	**Breads and Rolls, Yeast**	No (refrigeration makes bread go stale quickly)	2 to 3 months	In original package, then wrapped with foil or plastic wrap or in freezer bag
	Breads, Quick (such as banana bread, pancakes, or biscuits)	No (refrigeration makes bread go stale quickly)	2 to 3 months	In freezer bag
VEGETABLES	**Broccoli and Cauliflower**	3 to 5 days	8 to 12 months*	Blanched for 3 minutes, In freezer bag
	Cabbage (shredded or cut into thin wedges; for cooked dishes only)	1 week	8 to 12 months*	Blanched for 2 minutes, In freezer bag
	Carrots (cut into ¼ in. cubes)	2 weeks	8 to 12 months*	Blanched for 2 minutes, In freezer bag
	Corn (off the cob)	1 to 2 days	8 to 12 months*	Blanched for 3 minutes, In freezer bag
	Green Beans (trimmed)	1 week	8 to 12 months*	Blanched for 3 minutes, In freezer bag
	Potatoes, small (peeled)	No (they discolor and change flavor)	8 to 12 months*	Blanched for 3 to 5 minutes, In freezer bag
MEAT	**Steaks**	3 to 5 days	10 to 12 months	In freezer bag
	Chops	3 to 5 days	4 to 6 months	In freezer bag

WHAT TO SAVE	IN FRIDGE (set at or below 40°F)	IN FREEZER (set at or below 0°F)	HOW TO STORE IN FREEZER	
Roasts	3 to 5 days	10 to 12 months	In freezer bag	MEAT
Ground	1 to 2 days	3 to 4 months	In freezer bag	
Raw Sausages	1 to 2 days	1 to 2 months	In freezer bag	
Fully Cooked Sausages	Unopened, 2 weeks		In freezer bag (opened or unopened)	
Bacon	7 days	1 month (opened or Unopened)	In original packaging, placed in freezer bag	
Lean (such as cod, sole, flounder)	1 to 2 days	3 to 6 months	In freezer bag	FISH
Oily (such as salmon)	1 to 2 days	2 to 3 months	In freezer bag	
Shellfish (such as shrimp, shucked oysters, scallops, mussels, clams)	1 to 2 days	3 months	In freezer bag	
Whole	1 to 2 days	1 year	In freezer bag	POULTRY
Pieces	1 to 2 days	9 months	In freezer bag	
Ground	1 to 2 days	3 to 4 months	In freezer bag	
Grated Cheeses	1 month	3 to 4 months	In freezer bag	DAIRY
Blocks of Hard Cheese (such as Cheddar, Swiss, and Provolone)	Opened, 3 to 4 weeks Unopened, 6 months	6 months	Cut into smaller portions, each portion tightly wrapped in plastic wrap, then placed in freezer bag	
Soft Cheeses (such as Brie, not cream or cottage)	2 weeks	6 months	See Blocks of Hard Cheese, above	
Butter	2 to 3 months	6 to 9 months	For a month or less, in original packaging. For longer term, in freezer bag	
Egg Whites or Beaten Eggs; Egg Yolks	2 to 4 days	1 year (for egg yolks yolks mix with 1½ tsp. sugar or ⅛ salt per cup ¼ cup so yolks don't become sticky and gelatinous	In sealed container closest in volume to amount you're storing; label with numbers	

*To blanch vegetables, cook in rapidly boiling water for recommended time. Then cool quickly in ice water bath and drain well. This slows or stops the action of enzymes that can cause loss of flavor, color, and texture. Cook frozen vegetables without thawing.

TWO-WEEK BUDGET MENU PLANNER

WEEK 1

SUNDAY	Pot Roast with Fall Vegetables + mashed potatoes and gravy
MONDAY	Brisket Sandwiches (using leftover pot roast) + French Onion Soup + mixed green salad
TUESDAY	Spaghetti Bolognese (using leftover pot roast) + garlic bread
WEDNESDAY	Veggie Bean Burgers (using Home-Cooked Beans) + Baby Romaine with Fennel and Citrus (page 43)
THURSDAY	South of the Border Vegetable Hash (using Home-Cooked Beans) + bacon and eggs
FRIDAY	Chicken Tagine (made in a slow cooker) + toasted pita wedges
SATURDAY	Falafel Sandwiches + Greek Salad with Feta and Olives (page 43)

WEEK 2

SUNDAY	Apricot-Mustard Glazed Ham + mashed sweet potatoes + Spinach Soufflé
MONDAY	Ham Steak (using leftover ham) with Creamy Cheese Grits + fruit salad
TUESDAY	Multigrain Mac and Cheese with Creamy Tomato-Basil Sauce + steamed broccoli
WEDNESDAY	Split Pea Soup with Ham (using leftover ham) + biscuits
THURSDAY	Spring Ramen Chicken Soup + spring rolls
FRIDAY	Salad Niçoise + crusty bread
SATURDAY	Pastrami-Spiced Flank Steak (on the grill) + sliced rye + Carrot Coleslaw with Dried Cherries and Almonds (page 43)

INDEX

METRIC CONVERSION CHARTS

The recipes that appear in this cookbook use the standard United States method for measuring liquid and dry or solid ingredients (teaspoons, tablespoons, and cups). The information on this chart is provided to help cooks outside the U.S. successfully use these recipes. All equivalents are approximate.

METRIC EQUIVALENTS FOR DIFFERENT TYPES OF INGREDIENTS
A standard cup measure of a dry or solid ingredient will vary in weight depending on the type of ingredient. A standard cup of liquid is the same volume for any type of liquid. Use the following chart when converting standard cup measures to grams (weight) or milliliters (volume).

Standard Cup	Fine Powder (e.g. flour)	Grain (e.g. rice)	Granular (e.g. sugar)	Liquid Solids (e.g. butter)	Liquid (e.g. milk)
1	140 g	150 g	190 g	200 g	240 ml
¾	105 g	113 g	143 g	150 g	180 ml
⅔	93 g	100 g	125 g	133 g	160 ml
½	70 g	75 g	95 g	100 g	120 ml
⅓	47 g	50 g	63 g	67 g	80 ml
¼	35 g	38 g	48 g	50 g	60 ml
⅛	18 g	19 g	24 g	25 g	30 ml

USEFUL EQUIVALENTS FOR LIQUID INGREDIENTS BY VOLUME

¼ tsp	=							1 ml
½ tsp	=							2 ml
1 tsp	=							5 ml
3 tsp	=	1 tbls	=			½ fl oz	=	15 ml
		2 tbls	=	⅛ cup	=	1 fl oz	=	30 ml
		4 tbls	=	¼ cup	=	2 fl oz	=	60 ml
		5⅓ tbls	=	⅓ cup	=	3 fl oz	=	80 ml
		8 tbls	=	½ cup	=	4 fl oz	=	120 ml
		10⅔ tbls	=	⅔ cup	=	5 fl oz	=	160 ml
		12 tbls	=	¾ cup	=	6 fl oz	=	180 ml
		16 tbls	=	1 cup	=	8 fl oz	=	240 ml
		1 pt	=	2 cups	=	16 fl oz	=	480 ml
		1 qt	=	4 cups	=	32 fl oz	=	960 ml
						33 fl oz	=	1000 ml = 1 L

USEFUL EQUIVALENTS FOR COOKING/OVEN TEMPERATURES

	Fahrenheit	Celsius	Gas Mark
Freeze Water	32° F	0° C	
Room Temperature	68° F	20° C	
Boil Water	212° F	100° C	
Bake	325° F	160° C	3
	350° F	180° C	4
	375° F	190° C	5
	400° F	200° C	6
	425° F	220° C	7
	450° F	230° C	8
Broil			Grill

USEFUL EQUIVALENTS FOR DRY INGREDIENTS BY WEIGHT
(To convert ounces to grams, multiply the number of ounces by 30.)

1 oz	=	1/16 lb	=	30g
2 oz	=	¼ lb	=	120g
4 oz	=	½ lb	=	240g
8 oz	=	¾ lb	=	360g
16 oz	=	1 lb	=	480g

USEFUL EQUIVALENTS LENGTH
(To convert inches to centimeters, multiply the number of inches by 2.5.)

1 in	=			2.5cm
6 in	= ½ ft	=		15cm
12 in	= 1 ft	=		30cm
36 in	= 3 ft	= 1 yd	=	90cm
40 in	=			100cm = 1 m